SARPY COUNTY

· A HISTORY ·

BEN JUSTMAN

of the Sarpy County Museum

Published by The History Press
Charleston, SC
www.historypress.com

Cover image: Members of the Old Settlers group gather outside the First Presbyterian Church in Bellevue during one of their annual reunions. The Moses Merrill mission was the first religious presence in Sarpy County, shortly before it was burned in the 1930s. Today, only the chimney remains. *Sarpy County Museum.*

First published 2020

Manufactured in the United States

ISBN 9781467146562

Library of Congress Control Number: 2020941791

CONTENTS

ACKNOWLEDGEMENTS

This book is a continuation of efforts from previous Sarpy County historians and history-minded individuals. Their commitment and dedication to documenting our community history is critical, as new chapters of local history remain to be written. I would be remiss not to acknowledge their work, as well as The History Press for serving as a platform to help tell our expansive local history. I want to thank my fiancée, Jeannette, for her unwavering love and support. I am deeply grateful for a dedicated group of family, friends, museum volunteers and advocates who continue to offer their time, talents and goodwill.

INTRODUCTION

Sarpy County is small but mighty. At 240 square miles in area, 22 miles wide and 11 miles long, it is the smallest of Nebraska's ninety-three counties. The size of Sarpy County, however, is not relative to its expansive history, which stretches more than two hundred years.

Shortly after the Louisiana Purchase, Meriwether Lewis and William Clark stayed here in 1804 while charting the relative unknown in what would become the western half of the United States. Prior to their arrival, the indigenous peoples, primarily the Omahas but also the Pawnees and the Otoes, would have resided in the region. By the 1830s, the population consisted of a handful of fur traders and religious missionaries. One of these fur traders, Peter Sarpy, ran a successful operation at Bellevue. This trading post and ferry on the bank of the Missouri River would eventually become Nebraska's third-largest city.

Nebraska officially incorporated as a territory in 1854, and Bellevue became the gateway to the West for an influx of travelers. Many of them were on their way west for gold in California or in search of religious freedom in Utah. A number of travelers would ultimately stay in Bellevue, and with Sarpy as one of the organizers, the fledgling settlement went from trading post to town. Shortly after, on February 7, 1857, Sarpy County was established. All three of the first Sarpy County commissioners—John B. Glover, Robert McCarty and Philander Cook—were farmers. The first federal census taken in the young county just three years after its establishment indicated a population of 1,201 inhabitants.

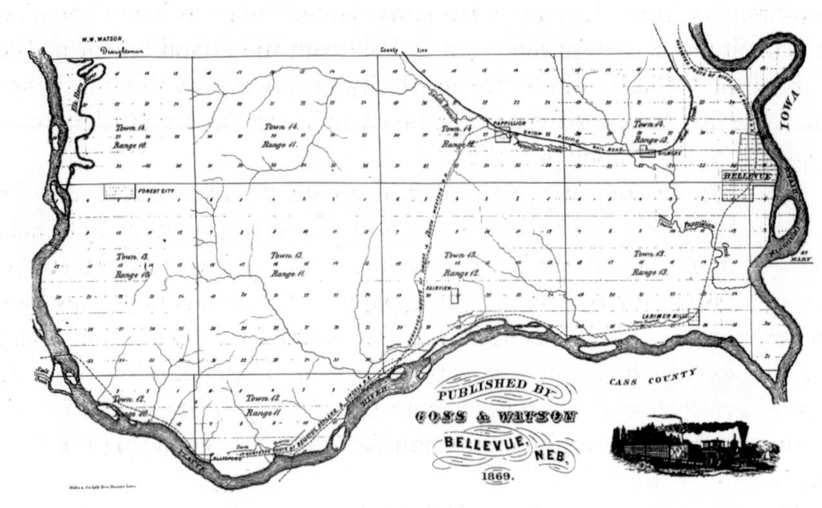

An 1869 map of Sarpy County displays mostly wide-open land, although some communities depicted no longer exist. *Sarpy County Museum.*

Whether spurred by the greater notion of Manifest Destiny or simply drawn to the prospect of farmland to call their own, pioneers in greater numbers than ever headed westward in the decades following the Civil War. New towns began to sprout. Papillion, Springfield and Gretna all have their origins associated with not only a sense of pioneer spirit and but also their connectivity to the railroad. Papillion's survived and thrived because the local residents, led by John Beadle, raised the necessary financial payment to convince Union Pacific to build in their fledgling town. Other towns such as Xenia, Portal and Chalco fell short in their effort to build a sustainable community and are now relegated to ghost town status. Sarpy Center, founded by Civil War veteran James Spearman, was unable to secure a railroad line to his young community. Rather than accept defeat, he hitched horses to most of the town's buildings and moved them a few miles to establish a new town. Thus, in 1881, the community of Springfield was born.

Bellevue was nearing extinction by the turn of the century. It had been passed over for both the territorial capital and the site of the transcontinental railroad, and its fur trade origins had become obsolete. The county courthouse had been relocated to Papillion in 1875, just five years after the town was founded. Much of the population in Bellevue had already left by that point, including Papillion's first mayor, William Robinson, as well as prominent Sarpy County judge James Gow. What was left of the oldest community in Nebraska managed to hold with the establishment in 1883 of Bellevue College, a four-year university, but its destiny forever changed when the first troops arrived at the newly built military installation known originally as Fort Crook in 1896.

By 1900, the county population had grown to 9,080, but for the first four decades of the twentieth century and despite its proximity to Omaha, change was gradual. It was in 1922 that the system of county prefix numbers was established for Nebraska license plates. The arrangement was based on the number of registered vehicles in the county at that time. Sarpy County was the fifty-ninth most populated of the ninety-three counties. The Roaring Twenties did little more than meow in Sarpy County, and as an agrarian community, the region faced hard times during the Great Depression of the 1930s.

With the coming of the Second World War, Sarpy County played a pivotal role in our nation's war effort. The Martin Bomber Plant at Fort Crook built more than two thousand bomber aircraft, including the planes that would drop the atomic bombs on Japan. At its peak in 1945, the facility employed more than fifteen thousand people. After the war, Fort Crook took on a new role. It was renamed Offutt Air Force Base and became home to Strategic Air Command. Thousands of military personnel and their families moved to Sarpy County. New neighborhoods, including Capehart and Wherry housing, were built to resolve a dire housing shortage.

The expanding role of the base had a significant impact on population, which more than tripled from 10,835 in 1940 to 31,281 by 1960. In addition to the oldest settlement in the state, Sarpy County is also home to Nebraska's newest community, La Vista, incorporated in 1960. Sarpy County now needed a new courthouse to accommodate this jet age surge of population, which between 1960 and 1970 had now more than doubled to 63,696. In 1974, the current courthouse structure was built, replacing the 1922 Classic Revival building that at present is home to Papillion City Hall.

Built on a solid historical foundation, Sarpy County continues to grow. The population is 181,000 residents and counting, with expectations that more than 317,000 will call Sarpy County home in 2050. From its humble beginnings to a thriving twenty-first-century urban landscape, Sarpy County has been on a remarkable journey, one with chapters that continue to be written.

This book contains but a select survey of a vast local history, and it seeks to improve the accessibility of our local history. An underlying theme of that remarkable journey is Sarpy County's connection, reaction and response to modernity. Another is how our local history is connected to larger events within the course of human history. Some of the narrative has previously been interpreted. Other aspects are vignettes from the community that have been forgotten, overlooked or under-considered. Ultimately, only so much can be accounted for between the front and back covers of a single book. As is with any volume highlighting historical past, it is hoped that future professional historians as well as lay armchair historians will consider digging deeper and proving further critical study of Sarpy County's rich history.

MANIFEST ON THE PRAIRIE

Many of the old-fashioned local histories place an overemphasis on historical firsts connected to Sarpy County. The first white child born in the Nebraska Territory, for example, is little more than a footnote. That being said, an early first that is not insignificant is Lewis and Clark's travels through the area. Having recently obtained nearly one-third of the continental landmass of the area that would eventually become the United States, President Thomas Jefferson commissioned Meriwether Lewis and William Clark to explore, map and find a viable route across the vast land mass. The two explorers and their small elite contingent known as the Corps of Discovery traveled through the great unknown during their expedition, which took place between May 1804 and September 1806. In late July 1804, the Corps of Discovery set up a camp near the mouth of the Platte River, where the unusually shallow and exceptionally wide river meets the confluence of the Missouri River. The camp, called Camp White Catfish, allowed the men to rest, make repairs to the keelboats and perhaps contact the indigenous Otoes. Writing in his now famous journal, William Clark indicated that he had "killed a deer in the prairie and found the mosquitos so thick and troublesome that it was disagreeable and painful to continue a moment still." It was not long before the Corps continued onward, but they utilized their old encampment during their return when they again passed through the area in 1806.

At the time, fur traders and missionaries found their way to Nebraska, the Omahas were led by Chief Big Elk, a well-liked politician who would have had to navigate potential warfare, disease and American encroachment. In his early days, he had established himself as a proven warrior during the War of 1812. But he was also a skilled negotiator, visiting Washington, D.C., in 1821 and 1837. Much of early Sarpy County history is intertwined, as further proven by the fact the Big Elk's daughter, Me-um-bane, married the fur trader Lucien Fontenelle. Both Lucien and Big Elk's grandson Logan would work for Peter Sarpy. Big Elk died in 1846. His hand-chosen successor was his adopted son, Joseph LaFlesche, a half-French, half-Ponca fur trader who likely lived in Bellevue's historic log cabin.

Born Pierre Gregoire Sylvester on November 3, 1805, Peter Sarpy was one of five children to Beral and Pelagie Sarpy. Beral had met Pelagie Labadie in France, and they were married in 1795. Departing for the New World shortly after, they made their way to St. Louis, a hub for commerce on the frontier. The Sarpys were related to many of the other influential families in St Louis, and it was not long before the family became fully vested in the fur trade business. Peter Sarpy, like his father and elder brother before him, entered the industry. He set off to the edge of the frontier to not only make his fortune but also prove himself as a man.

Sarpy would have arrived in Bellevue either in 1823 or 1824, when he was seventeen or eighteen years old. His brother's father-in-law, J. Cabanne, operated the trading post, and Sarpy, with his mix of education and upbringing, was given the position of clerk. Sarpy was described as what might come to mind for a typical man of French origin from the era: below medium height with black hair, a dark complexion and well-knit and a compact frame. His real prowess came not from his good looks but from his commanding attitude, language fluency and, when needed, specifically in the presence of the women, his polish and refined manner.

The majority of ferryboats along the upper Missouri were flatboats and skiffs with limited capacity. Unlike many of his contemporaries on the Missouri River, Sarpy by 1854 was utilizing a steam ferry, the *Nebraska*, to take travelers across the river. The March 21, 1855 issue of the *Nebraska Palladium* indicated that the boat was not a small craft, writing that it "had commenced her regular trips between St. Mary and Bellevue City. She was bought last year for thirteen thousand dollars and is altogether the largest and best ferryboat used on the Missouri River. She is of sufficient capacity to cross 25 or 30 teams at a time."

The ferry business could have its risks. The Missouri River was substantially wider and more rapid in the years prior to the Army Corps of Engineers' manipulation and management of the waterway. Even worse than rapids

Peter Sarpy, namesake of the county, helped to establish Bellevue and operated a successful trading post and ferry business across the Missouri River. *Sarpy County Museum.*

were wintertime ice jams, as was the case during the wintertime of 1855 when the Council Bluffs–Omaha ferry, the *General Marion*, sank in the river, leaving investors to turn to Peter Sarpy and his increasingly profitable ferryboat to transport migrants for the upcoming resurgence during the spring thaw.

In 1862, Sarpy moved to Plattsmouth with Nicomi, his native wife, turning his back on the town and county he helped to create. By this time, his empire had dwindled. His health was deteriorating, and his time in Plattsmouth only spanned a few years until his passing on January 4, 1865. After a brief burial, his remains were transported by steamer and reinterred at the family plot at St. Louis's Calvary Cemetery in July 1866.

Sarpy's death hardly received mention in the newspapers of the day, both in the Nebraska Territory and St. Louis. Rather, it was business as usual in Bellevue and Sarpy County. In fact, despite his death, there were still a number of debts and credits regarding the estate of Peter Sarpy that remained. Debts owed by Sarpy included $537.50 in delinquent taxes and a claim by Mills County, Iowa, for $1,175. A significant number of credits, far more than what Sarpy owed, were still outstanding to the estate, most of which were never collected.

Peter Sarpy could not have run his business ventures single-handedly. Among his business partners and employees was Lucien Fontenelle. Similar to Sarpy, Lucien was born in the New World but of French descent. His family had been in New Orleans for several generations when he was born in 1800. His childhood was abruptly cut short when both his parents died in a tremendous hurricane that struck the family home in Pointe Celeste while Fontenelle and his sister were attending school in New Orleans proper. The Fontenelle children lived with an aunt and uncle for several years and appear to have been financially taken care of. However, after a quarrelsome incident that reportedly involved a slap across the face for Fontenelle, the rebellious teenager set off for St. Louis and eventually Omaha in 1820.

Susceptibility to disease was a hazard of life in the eighteenth century. After a brush with death during a cholera outbreak in 1835, Lucien Fontenelle was once again struck by the sickness in 1839. The notable Belgian priest Father Pierre-Jean De Smet, who crisscrossed the country during his widespread missionary work, arrived in Bellevue shortly before the elder Fontenelle's death. Writing in his journal on February 6, 1840, he "arrived in Bellevue a few days ago just in time to administer the last sacrament to my old friend Lucien Fontenelle who died in my arms."

In addition to the indigenous population and a small contingent of fur traders, there would have been an even smaller number of missionaries in the Nebraska Territory. While Father De Smet was just passing through, others planted the flag of Christendom in the land mass that would one day be Sarpy County. In the fall of 1835, Moses and Eliza Merrill established their Baptist mission to teach Christianity to the local Otoe tribe located near the Platte River. Receiving $5,000 per year from the government, they had originally arrived in Bellevue in November 1833. For a while, they operated out of the nearby Indian Agency, but relations soured following their condemnation of the traders selling whiskey to the native population. They moved closer to the Platte River, near the Otoes. The husband-and-wife team constructed a small wood cabin with a large stone fireplace. A further three wooden structures would be built. To eventually provide shade, three cottonwood trees were planted, the last of which, long hollow, was removed in 2018.

The Otoe people did receive the missionaries, but it was with mild skepticism. The Otoes had their own language, customs and traditions and were not particularly interested in gravitating toward the King James Bible. Moses was, however, able to learn their language, and with that knowledge he translated several hymns, sections of scripture and a spelling book and reader from English into the Otoe language. After the better part of a decade on the isolated mission, Moses Merrill developed and quickly succumbed to consumption, more commonly known as tuberculosis. Before his passing, the thirty-six-year-old wrote in his diary that the Nebraska Territory was the "House of Satan and the Gate of Hell," but nonetheless, his last words were a prayer for someone to take his place after his passing. No one did. He was buried on the Iowa side of the Missouri River. The grave has since been washed away by the numerous occasions of the river flooding.

His wife and their young son did not stay for long, departing for St. Louis and abandoning the site. Nearly two hundred years later, all that remains of the first permanent mission in the Nebraska Territory is the large stone chimney, held up with the assistance of metal tension wires. Following the donation of the property from Dr. Jim and Inez Boyd to the Sarpy County Historical Society, Sarpy County made several improvements to the site and installed a fence around the perimeter. With improvements, the Mosses Merrill Mission site was placed in the National Register of Historic Places. The vast educational system in Sarpy County can trace much of its origins to the arrival of early missionaries seeking to bring their brand of salvation and education to the area's native peoples. Much of the work of these early missionary educators involved translating hymns and scripture passages for the Otoe, Omaha and Pawnee people.

By the time this photo was taken in the 1930s, the Moses Merrill Mission site was in rough shape. *Sarpy County Museum.*

In 1854, Nebraska became a territory, and not long after, Bellevue became an incorporated village. Early business and commerce in Sarpy County are typically associated with Peter Sarpy's trading post, but there is more to the story of course. Sarpy dealt in wholesale, selling to other businesses in addition to the selling of Indian goods, cattle, horses and mules. On May 30, President Franklin Pierce signed the Kansas-Nebraska Act and opened the Nebraska Territory to settlement. By 1857, the air was filled with the noise of hammers and saws. Stone foundations were put into place and hand-painted signs mounted, affixed to buildings. These signs advertised some of Bellevue's first business. This included Pike's Provision and Grocery Store. Located on Mission Avenue, east of Main Street, the store offered fresh groceries and a variety of liquors. It also had a restaurant in the back of the store that offered delicacies such as pickled tongue and tripe, pig's feet, sardines, wild game and several other options of the day.

Louis Bartels and Fritz Metz had a general store at Twenty-First and Main Street. Buffalo shoes and clothing, as well as liquors, medicines and varnishes (perhaps all one in the same), could be bought there, as could both window and china glass. While they bought produce from local farmers, they promoted that much of the stock came from St. Louis, as one of the partners was constantly there, searching for the highest-quality goods at the lowest prices to import to the Nebraska Territory. Not to be outdone, J.P. Horn's Variety Store was a competitor and offered, as the name implied, a variety of items. These included shovels, teakettles, horse collars, doors and tobacco, to name only a few. It was located near the newspaper office. A third general store, operated by W.M.C. Averill and Company, was also in Bellevue at this time.

Just as today, businesses closed or changed ownership. H. Cook Griffith's meat market, located under Pike's Grocery, was sold to George Oliver and Charles Stone. Griffith appealed to his customers to settle any outstanding debts owed both to him and to those he was required to pay as soon as possible.

Those with skills in the trade industry were common. Bellevue had a blacksmith and has had carpenters. Joseph Lowrie advertised that he could repair, varnish or custom make to order any piece of furniture. As was common, he could also produce a coffin in the shortest possible notice.

Before a trip to Lowrie, one hopefully might see William Longsdorf, MD, physician and surgeon, at his office on Main Street between Twenty-Fifth and Twenty-Sixth Streets. Longsdorf was young, in his early twenties, and did not have much experience, but he did have a college degree and was a graduate of a medical college, as well as dental school.

The first postmaster was Daniel Reed, and business was transacted in the old mission house on present-day Warren Street, between Nineteenth and Twentieth Avenues in Bellevue. Having a post office was significant. It was not only an outlet to the outside world, but it also further assisted in shoring up viability as a sustainable community by providing an opportunity to conduct business of the federal government. Reed had been serving in the capacity of acting postmaster since 1849, before Bellevue had even gained its name and was known to the traders, trappers and missionaries as Council Bluff. As a side note, Reed was also founder of Nebraska's first newspaper, the *Palladium*.

The *Nebraska Palladium*, and shortly thereafter the *Bellevue Gazette*, were printed on the Iowa side of the river and transported to Bellevue. An annual subscription to the *Gazette* was two dollars per year. There were numerous advertising options, ranging from one dollar for a one-time issue of a square of twelve lines or less, to sixty dollars for one year of column space. Henry M. Burt published the paper every Thursday. Found yourself needing legal representation? Bellevue had that as well, with at least five law firms operating with Bellevue connections. Need to spend the night to conduct business? The Bellevue House Hotel was a large structure and stood until it burned down in the twentieth century. Its owner, J.T. Allen, promoted "assiduous attention" to the wants of his guests.

The *Bellevue Gazette*, which superseded the *Palladium*, boasted that the newly minted county seat of Sarpy "in a short time will present a beautiful appearance, situated as the city is, on one of the handsomest plateaus on the Missouri River, whose high bluffs presents a barrier to that the ever-changing stream, through which it cannot break or overflow in all time to come. Let those who wish to seek a delightful home in the far west, visit this city." The people did come. Unfortunately, due to politics and Bellevue's early stumble, many would also leave not long after.

Sarpy County had been established by 1857, separating from once larger Douglas County. Residents in Bellevue felt that they were not properly being represented by their elected officials, who became increasingly invested both politically and economically in matters related to the budding city of Omaha. The matter was briefly debated in the territorial legislature before a vote in favor of a new county took place; with it, Sarpy County's formation arrived on February 1, 1857. Following independence, elected officials would be needed to steer the new county.

Was there ever a time when politics was not contentious? Historically, there never have been any "good old days" in the political arena. Since the first power struggle, there has always been that glimmer of gladiatorial combat. From recent presidential elections to the days of ancient kings, the battle to defeat an adversary has remained the same. For the first Sarpy County commissioners, that same determination likely held true as well.

Who were the first winners and losers to run for office in a race that would serve as the foundation for Sarpy County, its communities and its people? In the early years and well into the twentieth century, Sarpy County had just three county commissioners. The first three elected into office on May 25, 1857, were John B. Glover, Robert McCarty and Philander Cook. A fourth man, Reuben Lovejoy, rounded out the general ticket candidates but only received 74 votes to Cook's 141. Voter turnout was reported low, due to the farmers tending to their crops. To the winners went the privilege of political office, but just who were the trio of first Sarpy County commissioners?

Born in Connecticut, Philander Cook was one of the first settlers to enter the Nebraska Territory when the settlers crossed the Missouri River in 1854. Peter Sarpy and his ferry would have undoubtedly assisted them in the crossing. They made their home about four miles south of Bellevue and one mile west of the little town of La Platte. The Cook family's homestead consisted of 640 acres, half of which was wooded. Later, they took 75 acres and planted corn on the land, producing about three thousand bushels. Using the planting average of today, that same land would have provided more than thirteen thousand bushels of corn. Cook's son grew up in the vast openness and often played with the local native children. He grew up and later went on to become a very prominent businessman at Western Union.

Similar to Cook, Robert McCarty was also a farmer. Born in Decatur County, Indiana, in 1822, he was a veteran of the Mexican-American War and used his military land grant to obtain land in Iowa. When the Nebraska Territory was opened to settlers, he crossed the river and settled in September 1854. His first home was a log cabin. It would not be until ten years later that the family constructed a wood-frame farmhouse. Word of the benefits of the Nebraska Territory reached McCarty's brother Enoch, and he soon moved to Sarpy County as well. Both brothers were veterans and would often walk in their military greatcoats to South Omaha. Robert McCarty died in 1903 and is buried at Anderson Grove Cemetery. By then, his descendants called Sarpy County their home. Some still do.

John Bowen Glover, Sarpy County's final first county commissioner, was born in Kentucky in 1810. He bounced around, first relocating to Indiana and later Iowa before taking a chance on the Nebraska Territory. Records show that he lived in Sarpy County into the 1870s, but by 1880 he had moved to Louisville in Cass County. Similar to McCarty, Glover also erected a log cabin. The sixteen-by-twenty-foot dwelling used ten-foot logs. In addition to his occupation as a "merchant," Glover was a farmer, growing corn and pumpkins. He married Eliza Chase in 1831, and together they had at least nine children. He died in 1894 and is buried in Tabor, Iowa.

The issues these three men would have encountered probably would seem small compared to the debates and issues of the current county administration. None had much government experience, and it is difficult to imagine any of them as politicians, especially in the context of the world we live in today. Despite that, they all did share at least these traits: pioneering spirit and the willingness to get involved and potentially make a difference in one's community. Those traits were also shared by the first to be defeated in an election race for the position of Sarpy County commissioner, Reuben Lovejoy. Following his first failed attempt, he went on to become county commissioner and also became Bellevue's first mayor.

The mission to uphold law and order in Bellevue began long before the modern Bellevue Police Department was ever a consideration. In August 1858, William R. Watson, a farmer in his early forties, served as the first justice of the peace in Bellevue. He was joined by two constables, O.A.

Velie and N.W. Earls. In his position, Watson would have had far more authority than a modern-day police officer. A justice of the peace not only could apprehend an individual, but he could also oversee court and render a sentence as well. He could do all this with a limited legal education and in an ad-hoc courtroom that typically might be found in the back of a store or barbershop. It is unknown for certain how he would have interacted with the Sarpy County sheriff, established in Bellevue a year earlier in 1857.

It would be naïve to think that party politics connected to the national discourse have not historically been present in Sarpy County. Rather than the violent fury taking place in Bleeding Kansas, the majority of fighting in Nebraska was a battle of political wits. Bellevue and Sarpy County were in the pro-Union camp in the years leading up to and during the Civil War, especially when compared to the hotbed of Copperheads sympathetic to the Southern cause found in nearby Nebraska City. That said, there were still voices of dissent. Their stance was not necessarily directly aligned with proslavery views but rather in support of the 1856 political platform of the Democratic Party, which advocated for popular sovereignty, a means to let the population of a territory chose its own destiny regarding the question of slavery.

The infant Nebraska Territory needed leadership. The president of the United States, Franklin Pierce, selected William Orlando Butler of Kentucky to be the first territorial governor. The Mexican-American War general and vice presidential nominee of the 1848 declined. President Pierce's second choice was South Carolinian Francis Burt. The forty-seven-year-old Burt had been a loyal southern Democrat. He had voted in favor of nullification, South Carolina's first attempt to secede from the Union until reined in by President Jackson in 1833. At the time of his new appointment, Burt had been serving for the last few years as the auditor of the U.S. Treasury, prior to departing for the Nebraska frontier on September 11, 1854. The journey was a long four weeks of travel, and Burt was not a well man. Stomach ailments forced him to see a doctor in St. Louis, and by the time he arrived in Bellevue on October 7, he was confined to bed at the Presbyterian Mission House. With Burt in failing health, Judge Fenner Ferguson swore him in as Nebraska's first territorial governor on October 18. His tenure was short. Two days later, Burt succumbed to his sickness.

Bellevue's aspirations of serving as the site of the territorial capital eroded with the death of Burt. His successor, Thomas Cuming, a twenty-five-year-old from New York, had only been in his role as secretary of the Nebraska Territory for ten days when he assumed the role of acting governor. His time in office, lasting a little over four months, would be detrimental to Bellevue's sustainability and Sarpy County's early influence, as power and money resulted in the territorial capital being built in Omaha.

In 1860, Bellevue reported sixty-eight schoolchildren, a building valued at $600 and one male teacher, Henry A. Longsdorf, a relative of the elder Dr. Longsdorf. Small rural country schoolhouses sprang up elsewhere throughout the county to meet the needs of farmers and their children. Despite the children, by 1861, Bellevue would no longer be in the spotlight. The politics and money had moved north to Omaha. Both the bid to obtain the territorial capital and the transcontinental railroad had been lost. Some of the Bellevue businesses would close, their proprietors headed to greener pastures. Some, like accomplished businessman and philanthropist Henry T. Clarke, decided to stay and continue to call Bellevue home. Others heard the bugle call and decided to enlist in the army, as America was now at war with itself. Territorial differences of opinion faded into obscurity after the first shots of the Civil War were fired in 1861.

The old settlers of Sarpy County would hold an annual gathering, including these Bellevue pioneers seen circa 1900 at the Presbyterian church. *Sarpy County Museum.*

There are 138 known Union Civil War veterans buried in eleven different cemeteries throughout Sarpy County. The largest number in a single cemetery, 39, can be found at Bellevue Cemetery, followed by 30 at Fairview Cemetery. Of additional note, there is the case of Wick Ellis, the Confederate soldier whose grave can be found at Springfield Cemetery. Many, including Ellis, would come here in the years following the Civil War. Civil War veterans often became influential or civic-minded people in Sarpy County. County clerk and survivor of the notorious Andersonville Prison Louis Leiseur was a member, as was James D. Spearman, the founder of Springfield. Bellevue lawyer John Q. Goss belonged to the unit post and was its commander for a time. Other members included prominent farmers A.W. Trumble and William Ireland. They would actively participate in local chapters of the Grand Army of the Republic, a fraternal organization that sometimes is referred to as America's first interest group. In Sarpy County, there were three GAR chapters. The Dahlgren Post No. 55 was Sarpy County's first chapter, chartered on September 1, 1880. Post No. 106, the Kirkwood chapter, was based in Springfield and established in August 1882. Lastly, there was the youngest chapter, based in Gretna and established in 1889. Membership was limited to those who had served the Union during the war. Given that exclusivity, it should come as no surprise that over time their ranks thinned until the last man, John Lutz, died in 1934, thus closing the chapter of Sarpy County's Civil War history.

In 1856, a community was founded a few miles northeast of present-day downtown Papillion. Less than two weeks following the secession of the lower part of Douglas County to form Sarpy County, Papillion City was formally incorporated on February 13, 1857, gaining the distinction of becoming the first community christened in the new county. Not long after, however, Papillion City also gained the notoriety of becoming a ghost town, melting away into the landscape almost as quickly as it had come to fruition. That's not where our story ends though; rather, it serves as the prelude to the next 150 years of history.

Papillion City was not alone in its failure. It was extremely challenging for a new town to survive and thrive in this era. Following several significant setbacks, Bellevue's potential as a prosperous metropolis declined. For a time, it seemed destined to careen into obscurity as a once significant fur trading post that would now be relegated to a nearly forgotten little hamlet. Instead, following the Civil War, other communities—including a second attempt at Papillion—began to sprout out of the prairie.

The last Civil War veteran of Sarpy County, John Lutz Sr., died on December 30, 1934. Lutz came to Papillion in 1885 and was an active community member. *Sarpy County Museum.*

Prior to Papillion being platted as a viable town, there was the necessary business of securing the Union Pacific line. A town's viability in this era was often directly affected by its connectivity to a railroad. Courting the Union Pacific would have been quite a feat, in terms of both political and financial commitments. Early residents who enticed UP to build through their fledgling town collectively raised $1,200 to help convince the railroad that this was a worthy investment. Pledges came from twenty-nine individuals and ranged from a contribution of $5 to $400 from Dr. David Beadle.

The railroad investment was successful, and by year's end, the population had reached 333. The Papillion of today was officially platted on October 31, 1870. The original streets were 80 feet wide. The blocks, when full, were 280 feet square, with each lot 66 by 140 feet in size. A significant transformation from prairie to progressive city marked the early years for Papillion. While farming surrounded the city, commerce boomed, with early additions including the U.P. Mill (later on renamed the Papillion Roller Mill) and Sander's General Store.

To further solidify the establishment of Papillion, landowner Samuel Pike platted an adjacent area, known as Pike's Addition or South Papillion, in 1872; on paper, the community doubled in size. That same year, the first newspaper in Papillion, the *Sarpy County Sentinel*, was established. By 1874, it was facing competition as the first copies of *Papillion Times* rolled off the presses. The schoolhouse quickly became antiquated, and a large brick building was constructed in 1875. Part of that building has been incorporated into the current district office for the Papillion–La Vista Community Schools.

Five years had passed since the incorporation of the community by the Papio Creek. The dynamics of the region were changing, and Papillion stood to benefit, but it was not the only growing community in Sarpy County. With Bellevue a shell of its former self as a buzzing frontier town, debate ensued regarding the question of the county seat. A contested discussion occurred to relocate the county seat from Bellevue to either Papillion or Sarpy Center. Two rounds of voting ensued. Bellevue immediately lost. Sarpy Center, as the name aptly implied, had been established in 1874 with the primary intention of becoming the county seat. Its founder, James Dawson Spearman, a veteran of the Civil War, had placed the town in the midst of good roads and had attracted a hotel, a store and a blacksmith. The *Sarpy County Sentinel*, Papillion's other newspaper in addition to the *Times*, had also defected there in the midst of the county seat debate.

During the first round of voting, which had eliminated Bellevue, Sarpy Center had come out on top, beating out Papillion. When the second

The earliest known image of Papillion has two unknown men standing at the future site of Washington Street through downtown. *Sarpy County Museum.*

round of voting occurred on April 6, 1875, between the two remaining contenders, politicking through an organization called the Papillion Town Company helped to ensure that Papillion was in a stronger financial position to build the new courthouse. It was enough for Papillion to secure the courthouse election. Spearman's dream of creating a community was deferred. He hitched up the majority of the buildings in Sarpy Center and moved them down the road, closer to the railroad line, where he began a new community, Springfield.

Albert Sander had donated the land at the corner of First and Jackson Streets for the new Sarpy County Courthouse during the election. With the location and vote decided, the cornerstone dedication for the new forty-eight-feet-square two-story brick courthouse took place on July 3, 1875. Festivities included speeches, a free barbecue dinner and much cacophony from bands, rifle salutes and the firing of a cannon. Effective January 1, 1876, county government began operations in Papillion. The courthouse served the county for the next forty-seven years, until it could no longer keep up with the growth of the area. The reins of power were transferred to a new building, present-day Papillion City Hall.

Following the failed bid to obtain the courthouse, Sarpy Center founder James Spearman, as previously noted, moved the town's buildings to a more lucrative site in order to attract the railroad. On February 27, 1882, the new town plat was filed at the courthouse in Papillion. Less than one month later, the Missouri Pacific went through the new community of Springfield, Nebraska, and with land that Spearman contributed, the railroad built a twenty-four-by-fifty-foot depot.

Civil War veteran James D. Spearman founded Springfield following his failed bid to secure the railroad and courthouse in the ghost town of Sarpy Center. *Sarpy County Museum.*

With a rail line and now serving as a hub for commerce in much of western Sarpy County, Springfield grew at an accelerated rate, quickly dwarfing the bubbling spring of the town's namesake. There were three dry goods stores, four grocers, three hotels, a butcher, a bank, two lumberyards, two blacksmiths, one saloon, two churches and a litany of other smaller shops for the three hundred residents. James Spearman's vision of a sustainable community was further solidified when Springfield was incorporated on January 4, 1884.

The same year that Springfield found its way onto the map, Bellevue was simply attempting to stay on the map. Nearly relegated to ghost town status, Bellevue's survival would depend on the metaphorical sword and pen representing Fort Crook and Bellevue College. Education would, in part, hold the keys to not only success but also the community's survival. "Open to both sexes. Tuition low. Location Beautiful and Healthful. Only nine miles from Omaha on the Burlington Railroad"—found immediately below an advertisement for McCarthy and Burke Undertakers, that's how the sales pitch for Bellevue College read in August 1883.

Organized three years earlier in 1880 by the Nebraska Synod of the Presbyterian Church, the first freshmen class consisted of twenty-six students. Educational offerings increased over time, but coursework was fairly typical of its day. Classical and modern languages, literature, mathematics, astronomy, mental and moral science, music, natural science and didactics were all taught at the school by an educated faculty. Postgraduate degrees were added, and the school further awarded forty-one master's degrees and thirty-seven doctorates. College expenses listed in 1885–86 were $140 per academic year. That may sound reasonable, but take into consideration that the budget in 1890, according to Dr. Kerr, the college president, was $4,660. A reliance on fundraising and donors helped to ensure that the school's finances finished in the black during much of its existence.

The first structure, and home to the administration, was Clarke Hall, built in 1883 at a cost of $20,000 and named in honor of Bellevue philanthropist H.T. Clarke. The campus steadily grew over the years. Rankin Hall, built in 1895, housed the college president. Finlay Hall, a dormitory, later burned down and was replaced by Fontenelle Hall in 1903. A popular location on campus, Fontenelle also housed the school's cafeteria in its basement. Built in 1897, 1900 and 1901, respectively, Philadelphia Hall, Lowrie Hall and Hamilton Hall were all primarily dormitories for the student body. Rounding out the college was a gymnasium built on Old Elk Hill in 1916.

The college had an active student body, both male and female. Many students were from the Sarpy County communities or Omaha. Others came from throughout Nebraska. A closer look at the 1917 student body shows that pupils came from nine different states. There was even the

Built in 1883, the main building at Bellevue College, Clarke Hall, housed classes, a chapel and a school library. It was torn down following World War II. *Sarpy County Museum.*

occasional exchange student from Japan and the Philippines. One unique alum found in the school annuals was Russel Taylor, class of 1896. Taylor was the school's first and possibly only African American student. He went on to become a Presbyterian minister, early civil rights advocate and a prominent member of the Omaha black community in the early 1920s. Before he relocated to Omaha, Taylor took his ministerial skills to the unique African American town of DeWitty, Nebraska, in Cherry County and filed a homestead claim.

Long before Title IX was passed, women partook in athletics at Bellevue College. The school offered a girls' basketball team and credit-bearing physical education courses. Men had the option of baseball, football, tennis and track. Hastings College, Doane College and Creighton University were all common opponents. The school colors were purple and gold, perhaps serving as the point of origin for the purple currently used by Bellevue Public Schools. For those seeking something less physically taxing, there were numerous student organizations. These waxed and waned through the years but typically included literary and oratorical associations, musical clubs and religious societies.

By 1907, Bellevue Public Schools had elected to dissolve its ninth and tenth grades, as the college provided these opportunities. The only problem was that Bellevue College would ultimately shutter its doors. For a few years following the closure of the college, high school classes continued in the empty buildings until 1921, when that no longer became an option; Pioneer High School, as it was called, was forced to vacate.

Despite the success of Bellevue College in the last two decades of the 1800s and even into the early years of the 1900s, by World War I, the school was facing trouble. A thinning student population, accelerated by military-aged males; a lack of significant local support; and the Presbyterian Synod's decision to refocus its financial efforts to Hastings College all led to the closure of Bellevue College in 1917.

The college was gone, but not the educational drive. The buildings housed Pioneer High School until 1921. It also briefly served as a vocational school for reentering civilian life after the war. In the years that followed, a number of the abandoned buildings suffered from dilapidation and were razed. Others were given a second chance and turned into apartments in the years leading up to World War II. At present, only three buildings remain from this once vast and picturesque college campus. Its impact has largely been forgotten, as have been the driving individuals who made the school possible, namely Henry Tefft Clarke.

Henry Tefft Clarke laid out the town of Bellevue, built its first schoolhouse, constructed the town's depot and aided in establishing Bellevue College. *Sarpy County Museum.*

H.T. Clarke arguably did more for Bellevue in the pioneer years than any other individual. It was in Bellevue that he and his brother started a general merchandise and supply store outfitting oxen trains going west. Their business expanded in 1856, when the Clarke brothers became steamboat agents at Bellevue.

In 1862, they contracted with the government for oats, corn and other supplies for Fort Kearney, two hundred miles to the west. In 1864, they commenced commercial freighting from Bellevue to Denver. There were twenty-seven teams employed consisting of five to seven yoke oxen, with two wagons to a team. It would have been quite an operation. By comparison, records show that during this time, the government paid a claim of $9,350 for eighty-five oxen to the Sioux.

Spurred by these early successes, in 1864 H.T. Clarke tried to secure the eastern terminus of the Union Pacific at Bellevue. When that failed, he coordinated efforts to have Omaha and Southern build a track to Bellevue. The 1869 railroad depot built for the line still stands in Bellevue's Gemini Park and is the oldest surviving train station in Nebraska.

At about this time, A.W. Clarke bought his brother's interest in the Bellevue store and eventually relocated to Papillion. There the Clarke brothers continued to make a positive difference within the community. H.T Clarke, an astute businessman, began building bridges all over the Platte River. Seven bridges were built, aiding America's expansion westward and cashing in on the discovery of gold in the sand hills of South Dakota. Clarke's bridge building ties even made it into Mari Sandoz's book *Miss Morissa: Doctor of the Gold Trail*, where he served as one of the based-on-true-life characters. His business investments ultimately spanned across the territory and later the state, from Bridgeport to Schuyler and Omaha, but they began in Bellevue.

In addition to his business ventures, he was active in numerous community endeavors, including the Nebraska Territorial Pioneers Association, and was elected president of the Nebraska State Historical Society in 1906. A generous man, H.T. Clarke gave 265 acres of land to the Presbyterian Church in 1882 and constructed the first building for Bellevue College. It was named Clarke Hall in his honor. The school was a major investment for Bellevue during its bleak years and was one of two significant factors—the other being the construction of a military installation—that ensured the community did not fade away as a forgotten nineteenth-century town.

Clarke lived about a dozen years into the twentieth century, passing away in 1913. He is buried at Forest Lawn Memorial Park Cemetery in Omaha. Notice of his death was announced in newspapers across the nation and in business publications. The building that bore his name at Bellevue College was demolished in 1946; his commitment and dedication were now gone from the landscape.

Bellevue College was one of two occurrences that solidified Bellevue and Sarpy County's history and relationship with the military. The origins of that history begin in the year 1887. In Paris, construction of the Eiffel Tower had begun. Gottlieb Daimler unveiled his horseless carriage—you may know it as the automobile. While stateside, in Nebraska, the population of Omaha had reached thirty thousand people. However, the story of Fort Crook, present-day Offutt Air Force Base, doesn't begin in Nebraska. Instead, one of the last of the frontier forts began inconspicuously as a bill on Capitol Hill, introduced by Senator Charles F. Manderson and signed into law by President Grover Cleveland the following year on July 23, 1888.

What we now know as Offutt AFB was built in the early 1890s as Fort Crook, an army post. Authorization to build the fort was limited to "not more than 1,000 acres in Sarpy, Washington, or Douglas County"—ultimately, a site near the little village of Bellevue was chosen. The first land was purchased in 1889, a tract of land consisting of 502.59 acres bought for $122.17 per acre. An additional 43.08 acres of land were purchased that same year, bringing the total to 545.67 acres.

Named in honor of the late General George Crook, construction of the fort took more than five years; it was ready for occupancy in 1896. Its namesake, General Crook, was an accomplished veteran of both the American Civil War and later the Indian Wars. Friend and foe alike respected Crook. The Apaches dubbed him "Grey Wolf," while President Rutherford B. Hayes named his own son George Crook Hayes. Despite his actions on the battlefield, where he fought Crazy Horse and Geronimo, among others, Crook spent his later years speaking out against the ill treatment of Native Americans. In 1879, he testified on behalf of the Ponca Tribe during the trial of Standing Bear, when a federal judge determined that an Indian was due the rights and privileges of man. While serving in

Following their departure from Fort Keogh in Montana, the first men of the Twenty-Second Infantry Regiment arrived with their families at Fort Crook in 1896. *Sarpy County Museum.*

Chicago, Crook passed away suddenly at the age of sixty-one in 1890. He is buried at Arlington National Cemetery.

Five years may seem like a long time to construct a smattering of buildings, but the Quartermaster Corps had to take into account freshwater wells, sewer systems, roads and building materials, all of which had to be thought out in great detail prior to the arrival of the first garrison troops, an advance party of ten enlisted men led by a second lieutenant on a warm summer day in late June 1896.

When the Twenty-Second U.S. Infantry Regiment was ordered to Cuba in 1898 to participate in the Spanish-American War, only 41 enlisted men and 2 officers remained behind to garrison Fort Crook. The Twenty-Second would battle the Spanish at San Juan Hill, alongside Teddy Roosevelt's Rough Riders and regiments of Buffalo Soldiers. During the battle, Colonel Charles A. Wikoff, commander of the Twenty-Second, was mortally wounded. Prior to departing for Cuba, Wikoff had resided in Quarters 16 of Officers' Row. The regiment suffered many casualties in addition to Colonel Wikoff, with only 165 men and officers from the original cadre of 513 returning to Fort Crook in September 1898. Most of the losses were the result of deaths or discharges due to the effects of tropical diseases such as malaria. Some of the troops who returned to Nebraska continued to fight illnesses, and those who died were buried at the post cemetery.

Veterans of Cuba would join many additional new recruits as the Twenty-Second Infantry Regiment rebuilt its strength at Fort Crook prior to its deployment in the Philippine Insurrection the following year. They would once again return to Fort Crook in 1902, only to redeploy a second time to that conflict in 1903, but by then the military post near the small but persistent town of Bellevue had been well established.

Other towns in Sarpy County did not have the equivalent of a Bellevue College or Fort Crook to spare them from obsolescence. There have been thirty-one different post offices throughout Sarpy County, an indicator of where people lived, how they migrated and how many communities have been relegated to ghost town status. A few such towns are Larimer, Chalco and Portal.

Portal was not a gateway into another dimension; instead, it was, for a time, a successful community. In an era when connectivity to the railroad was often vital for success, Portal was a junction for two rail lines: the Union Pacific and Missouri Pacific Railroads. Additionally, the Burlington ran on the edge of town. Located near present-day 108th and Giles Road, the town would have been west of Papillion by about two miles. Platted in 1887, Portal was slated to be the next big community; however, it ultimately stalled out. The fifty inhabitants of the chiefly industrial town operated a farm implement factory that produced harrows, a tool used to help break up soil. There was also a steam cooker factory, a grain elevator and a section house full of railroad men. Rounding out the town were two saloons, one German Methodist church, a general store and a hotel. A schoolhouse was built in 1888 for District 22, and Portal School would continue to operate for close to one hundred years after the town reverted back to farmland. Today, only the cemetery and the relocated schoolhouse remain.

Larimer, the earliest of the three aforementioned ghost towns, was located four miles south of Bellevue, at the confluence of the Platt and Missouri Rivers. Within a year of the opening of the territory to pioneers, a plan was conceived to develop a town. A small, influential group of four men—Territorial Governor Thomas Cumming; Territorial Treasurer Benjamin Rankin; Richard Hogeboom, a farmer and Black Hawk War veteran; and prominent railroad tycoon William Larimer—served as principals of the town project. It never got any further than a tavern and sawmill and was given the name La Platte before it was abandoned for higher ground away from the floodplain in early 1856. In the wake of defeat, a new town was surveyed and platted. Larimer (sometimes known as Larimer City) was described as being

> *located upon an extensive and beautiful plateau, directly at the junction of the Platte and Missouri Rivers. This plateau is considerably elevated above the Missouri River, sloping gradually towards it, and admirably situated for a large business metropolis. The plateau is bounded on the east and south by these two rivers, on the north by the Papio Creek and on the west, by a gradually sloping prairie, which rises to a level with the upland lying west of the plateau. This plateau is about two square miles in extent and embraces as beautiful a tract of land, lying toward the rising sun, as can be found in the world.*

Despite holding the high ground, the second incarnation would fail too. The post office lasted two years before being discontinued, and the town withered away. Remaining buildings would be absorbed into a third town in 1870, the second incarnation and present-day hamlet of La Platte. Larimer would not let this setback deter him. He continued westward, where he would become the founder of another, far more successful town: Denver, Colorado.

The final of the three ghost towns in focus, Chalco, was an 1888 railroad town developed northwest of Papillion. The well-known recreation area that inherited the town's name has helped to keep the unusual title in the public lexicon, but little is known of the small community. While the town is gone, the area still remains as a census district. Despite the rural post office remaining until 1950, the once largely German American community was prone to flooding and ultimately had trouble growing beyond its initial boom. Further damage to the town came when its only financial institution, the German American Chalco State Bank, was closed by the State of Nebraska in 1918 due to the incompetency of its officials after mismanagement resulted in the loss of more than $26,000. The bank had purchased $36,000 worth of notes from the Mutual Benefit Health & Accident Association but was only able to collect on $10,000 worth of the notes. The small-town bank declared that it was not responsible and called on the association's treasurer, C.C. Criss, to resign. Judgment was not ruled in its favor, and the bank fell apart, as did any chance of the survival of the town. Criss, however, thrived and eventually

Sarpy County has more than a few ghost towns, like Chalco, possibly seen here following the 1903 flood. Little remains of most of these communities. *Sarpy County Museum.*

went on to become the CEO of Mutual of Omaha for twenty years, his legacy continuing through a foundation and the Dr. C.C. and Mabel Criss Library at the University of Nebraska–Omaha.

Given America's greater vision of Manifest Destiny and with the steady flow of immigrants settling in the heartland, it was only a matter of time before western Sarpy County attracted new inhabitants. Today, western Sarpy County is synonymous with the community of Gretna, but early events in this region predate Gretna by roughly thirty years. The origins of this area can be linked with the now ghost town of Forest City. Located near the Elkhorn and Platte Rivers, Forest City was incorporated on April 18, 1858. The community makeup would have been predominately Irish. Due to the dense woods nearby, most of the homes and structures would have been earthen dugouts or log cabins, including the church for the overwhelmingly Catholic community.

Forest City was a budding town containing a post office, two stores, multiple saloons, a blacksmith shop, a shoemaker and two boarding homes. The town had been conveniently located near the main road to Omaha and Ashland and eventually to Lincoln, and in the early years, Forest City dominated much of the crossing of the mighty Platte River and travel scene. What Forest City did not have, however, was a railroad.

When the Burlington Railroad constructed a line between Omaha and Ashland, the town inhabitants slowly drifted away to be closer to the prosperity of the tracks.

Gretna was not founded on the folksy romanticism of a frontiersman or pioneer but rather by developers. The Lincoln Land Company frequently collaborated with the Burlington Railroad to build towns along routes. It purchased eighty acres of land at a total cost of $560 from the State of Nebraska and surveyed and platted the land with the Sarpy County clerk on August 6, 1886. A depot was quickly built, followed by grain elevators. By July 10, 1889, when Gretna was formally incorporated, the majority of Irish formerly from Forest City, along with a wave of Pennsylvania Dutch families, were now calling Gretna home.

Echoing a narrative similar to many other towns, the first business was a general store. In Gretna, that would be Gus and Clem McKenna's general store. Gus McKenna was also the town's first postmaster. The Forest City Catholic Church had relocated to Gretna. Its congregants dedicated their church, St. Patrick's, in 1895.

Built at a cost of $8,000, Gretna completed a seven-room school, four of which were classrooms in 1898. Declared too small just ten years after its construction, an addition doubling the size of the building was constructed in 1908. Steam furnaces kept the building warm during the cold months, but until plumbing was installing in the late 1920s, the matching "his" and "hers" outhouses were located behind the all-brick school building. A gymnasium would eventually be added in 1936. Also of note, Gretna was the first district in Nebraska to utilize school buses. These were two large horse-drawn enclosed carriages that traveled three and a half miles for eleven students and four and one fourth miles for another twenty-three pupils.

It is important to note that at one time there were forty different school districts within Sarpy County—simply too many to cover within this book. Districts 37 and 14 served Gretna-area residents. School District 22 consisted of Portal School, while Sautter School was in District 15. Stringtown, more formally known as District 9, could be found in the southwestern part of the county. Many of these districts served rural areas of the county and were one-room schoolhouses with all grades and a single teacher. Schools such as Prairie Queen, Portal and Bell Schools are just a few of these. There were a few larger schools: Fort Crook had a four-room schoolhouse, and District 5 covered the Avery area, which had several different schools. Over time, these districts and dozens more consolidated to better serve the residents of Sarpy County, both in Gretna and within the other communities.

Gretna resembles a Wild West Hollywood set in this early circa 1880s photo. Peters Hardware, Knoll's Commercial Hotel and Hughes Brothers Store were all early businesses. *Sarpy County Museum.*

Gretna was the last community to be established in Sarpy County before the U.S. government in 1890 announced the closure of the western frontier, meaning that there were no known tracts of land that did not already contain settlers. By 1900, Sarpy County had transformed from the hardscrabble pioneer experience emblematic of westward wagons to that of a relatively quiet hardscrabble farming landscape. For years, the Old Settlers Picnic was attended by many of the old families every summer. By the 1910s, the death list published between annual meetings had become expansive; eventually, the Old Settlers outing had to be combined with Douglas County's before finally numbering too few to celebrate.

CHANGING TIMES

Modernity in Sarpy County

In similar fashion to Thornton Wilder's three-act play *Our Town*, life in Sarpy County went on. There was love, marriage and death. In between, the farmers farmed and children went to country schools or attended one of the schools in town. Dances and celebrations were occasionally held. Public officials met and discussed how to better the county and towns. Not included in Wilder's play but an essential aspect throughout Sarpy County was the effort by the more managed communities to focus on sustaining and building their infrastructure. It has not always been as simple as the turn of a faucet. Plumbing, pipes and civic projects had to be installed to connect and bring Papillion into the modern world.

The first attempt at this was little more than a hole in the ground. In 1896, the city dug a well for visitors and their horses who came to town. Presumably prior to that, townsfolk and guests alike would have routinely gone to the nearby Papillion Creek. The first documented offering of publicly available water through the municipality was during a July heatwave in 1898. The county commissioners installed a ten-gallon tank in the hall of the courthouse, offering free drinking water to the public. Clean drinking water was not only a way to stay hydrated on a warm summer's day but also essential toward the betterment of public health in order to curtail disease.

The addition of a municipal waterworks was far from unanimous, but it did have both a large and vocal majority. In March 1907, the motion to construct a waterworks facility easily passed by a vote of 105 to 33. Led by James Spearman, Papillion businessman and relative to the founder of Springfield, a celebratory bonfire was held and three rousing cheers were made to commemorate the milestone.

Undoubtedly, they were celebrating the accessibility to clean, fresh drinking water and not the $18,000 price tag. The contract was awarded to Omaha city engineer George W. Craig for the 105-pound-pressure waterworks, and by the time work was completed, the cost had naturally increased, such is often the case related to modernity and progress.

A staple in Papillion until its demise in 1961, the old water tower filled the skyline after its construction in 1907. With the approval of the waterworks and the tower, it seemed that water would flow from the faucets of Papillion, but the battle was just heating up.

It took more than a year for the water system to go into operation due to a reported disagreement with the contractor over the well. It was reported that during the second week of December, the steam pump ran continuously to bring water up from the well, but with little effect. By the following week, it had been determined that the well had collapsed in on itself. Even with technological advancement in place, progress was not producing.

In March 1908, an expert from Kansas City was lowered into the well to determine if it was necessary to dig an entire new well or if they could finish completing the original well. The quicksand that was found required the city to dig a new well and spend another $500 in the process.

Progress did ultimately pay off, and in May 1908, Tom Boyer became the first individual in Papillion to have city water installed. It was reported that a number of other businesses and residences would have water installed, as soon as Water Commissioner William Saalfeld was able to do so.

In October 1910, the first public outdoor drinking fountain was erected in the square, northwest of Sander's store at Second and Washington Streets. Residents made use of the water fountain and the clean running water. To accommodate the sharp rise of residents utilizing the city's water, a new pump house and expansion of the city's waterworks facility were completed in the summer of 1915.

Papillion would join the ranks of New York, London and Paris on Monday, November 15, 1909, when a switch was pulled, and thirty eighty-watt tungsten incandescent lights were turned on, brightening key points throughout the main strip of Papillion. Curious residents went from light to light, investigating the technology and the illuminating difference the lights made to the streetscape. The lights were made possible by the passing of Village Ordinance 121 the previous year.

This would have spelled doom for the town lamplighter, eliminating any job security for the man responsible for the daily manual lighting and occasional cleaning of the glass globes. In 1897, that would have been a new hire by the name of Jack Welsh, ironically bearing the same name but not related to the former General Electric executive. Prior to that, the town marshal was paid an extra ten dollars per month to light the lamps. By comparison, Bellevue had only gained thirteen gas streetlamps in December 1904, and before that achievement, individuals stumbled around in the darkness, utilized a hand-held lantern or simply had no business going outside once the sun set.

The first to further capitalize on electricity for marketing purposes was R.E. Tallon, the owner of the Sarpy House Hotel. In January 1911, Tallon installed an electric sign on the corner of the building, flicking off and on in the darkness.

Telegraph poles, later used for the telephone, are visible in many early photographs of Papillion. They would have already been in place in many instances for stringing further electrical wiring. The modernization was not exclusive to Papillion, as the Bellevue Village Board approved for the Home Telephone Company and any of its successors to construct poles and wires in December 1901. The first known invoice to appear in the Village of Bellevue's bills for use of the telephone appeared in the April 8, 1902 meeting minutes and was to the tune of seventy-five cents.

The residents of Papillion were probably just becoming accustomed to illumination when disaster struck in 1913, plunging the town into darkness. While Papillion was physically unharmed from the Easter tornado of 1913, Ralston was obliterated, including the powerhouse that brought electricity to the village. It took nearly a month before power was restored to residents.

In the summer of 1915, downtown Papillion received a little extra pizzazz when strings of electric lightbulbs and Japanese lanterns added not only an extra layer of decoration but also a sense of metropolitan modernity.

Sarpy County at one time was home to not one but two streetcar lines. One of these went through downtown Papillion on Eighty-Fourth Street. The other connected Bellevue to Omaha. By the turn of the twentieth century, Bellevue had received a new lease on life. Following its failed bid to obtain the Nebraska territorial capital and the transcontinental railroad, there had been some questionable years when the one-time fur trading community might have decomposed back into the Nebraska landscape. However, with the founding of Bellevue College and the establishment of Fort Crook, Bellevue had found its place. Capitalizing on this stability, the Omaha Interurban Trolley Company decided in 1906 to extend its service, which had previously terminated in South Omaha, to the army post, with several stops along the route.

The proposed line would have started in South Omaha at Twenty-Fourth and North Streets and proceeded down Twenty-Fourth Street and across the present-day Kennedy Freeway, where it ran parallel and west to Bellevue Boulevard. Eventually, the route crossed onto Harvell Drive, passed Dowding Pool and underneath fifty-five feet below the aptly named "Suicide Bridge," where it dumped into Olde Towne, crossing diagonally at Washington and Nineteenth Streets.

The interurban stops would have included some familiar names, such as Avery, Jewel Place, Childs, Bellevue College and Fort Crook. Cars could also be charted by groups for special occasions, such as church groups or troops from Fort Crook on their way north to take part in the Ak-Sar-Ben parade. The cost of a regular fare varied, but it was broken into three zones, costing $0.10 to Bellevue and an additional $0.05 to Fort Crook. For regular riders, there was the option of buying a booklet of twenty tickets for $1.50.

The rolling stock for the Bellevue line primarily consisted of two streetcars, with infrequent use of a third. The forty-one-foot cars weighed roughly twenty tons and reportedly could hold between forty-four and fifty-four passengers. Beautiful woodwork of mahogany and oak would have adorned the interiors, which were both heated and illuminated. Similar to the surviving car at the Durham Museum, the streetcars on the Bellevue line were yellow. Maximum speeds were thirty miles an hour, and the span of the line could be covered in about eighteen minutes provided there were no stops. The vast majority of streetcars did not have the cowcatcher or fender device used to soften the blow against an animal or human. In the bustle of Omaha, that would have meant doom for a wayward pedestrian, but in Bellevue, the streets were largely free and clear—not only due in part to a sparser population but also because Bellevue had modernized two years prior to the arrival of the streetcar when, in 1904, the village board passed a resolution to "prohibit the running of large cattle, horses, mules, sheep, goats, or swine and restricting the herding of cattle upon the streets avenues, or public ground of the Village of Bellevue." With modern twentieth-century comforts, the streetcar would have been a great method of travel for those without either a horse or a horseless carriage or for those who did not want to wrangle with Bellevue's notorious dirt roads.

By the late 1920s, the times had changed. Bellevue College had closed. Fort Crook remained established but was in the relative tranquility of the interwar period. The Roaring Twenties did not fully extend to Bellevue,

Nebraska. With Bellevue's population at nearly three thousand people, there just wasn't enough activity to sustain a profitable streetcar line. Increased automobile usage further negated the line's purpose. In 1930, the company reported a loss of $30,000—a final blow to the hemorrhaging Omaha and Southern, which had reported losses for some time. By the following year, the hum of the streetcar motor and clang of its bell ceased in Bellevue and were replaced with buses in attempt to streamline and modernize the operation.

A few small tokens of the streetcar days remain, but not much beyond that. The Sarpy County Museum has a restored waiting shelter for the Bellevue Boulevard stop and a few photographs of the line. The streetcar station at Nineteenth and Washington still remains, albeit as a private residence. Another structure that once served as a ticketing station for the streetcar is now part of an auto body shop on Fort Crook Road. A few places remain where the streetcar right of way can still be seen before it erodes back into the landscape.

With utilities and public transit modernizing the landscape, it was only natural that twentieth-century technology, especially the automobile, began to appear. Perhaps one of the earliest documented automobiles to take to the streets in Sarpy County was that of accomplished photographer Louis

The streetcar came through both Papillion and Bellevue and provided greater connection to Omaha than the questionable roads. Photo circa 1913. *Sarpy County Museum.*

Bostwick of Omaha. His visit to Papillion in 1901 brought crowds of curiosity seekers out onto Washington Street. Bostwick was greeted by Mayor Charles Rosencranz, while Papillion resident Charles Hagedorn and Rosencranz's son, David, received a ride in the steam-powered Locomobile.

In May 1911, a number of auto owners donated their rides for a fundraising benefit. At ten cents per ride, Emil Grothe, I.D. Clarke, Sam Arbuthnot, H.P. Beerline, Mike Zwiebel and half a dozen other men drove one of three different routes, offering tours of Papillion from an automobile. It is unknown how much money was raised, but it can be safely assumed that this opportunity provided many local residents a first chance to ride in a motorized vehicle.

In November 1911, the unique group of automobile owners organized a formal club, meeting at the Sarpy County Courthouse. E.G. Fase was elected the president of the club, which initially had about twenty-five owners. Dues were rather steep at $1.25 per year. That same year, the newspaper still contained advertisements for local horse whisperers and blacksmiths, including A.W. Critchfield's shop, which offered horseshoeing and carriage work.

Horse and wagon were still the predominant method of transportation in Sarpy County, but by June 1914, the *Papillion Times* was reporting that the purchase of a new automobile (a significant event not long before) had become so commonplace that the story of a new acquisition was no longer newsworthy. What was newsworthy in November 1915 was an early case of vehicular vandalism, if not the first for Papillion. Resident Ed McCarthy had the windshield, horn, two extra tires and an overcoat taken from his Ford, which had been stored in a shed. The culprit still remains unknown, although he or she is presumably no longer at large.

The advancement in technology did not come without incident. These early autos were prone to poor handling, weak wheel traction and instability. In one such incident in May 1915, the car carrying outgoing Bellevue mayor John Freeman flipped while traveling down the Bellevue Boulevard. Both occupants were pinned underneath the vehicle; his passenger was able to crawl out and lift the car so that he was able to crawl out. Freeman escaped with his life and little lament. Damage to the car was estimated at seventy-five dollars. He was one of the lucky ones.

As Sarpy County modernized over the course of several decades, the waxing and waning of life took place. Life was quiet, even idyllic, marred only by the occasional significant event. The fire of 1903 in Springfield would be one such occurrence. By this time, Springfield was firmly entrenched, with

The 1901 Bostwick visit to Papillion. It was written that "several mules could scent an automobile as soon as it crosses into Sarpy County." *Sarpy County Museum.*

an established downtown that lined both sides of Main Street. Shortly after midnight on March 19, 1903, a fire started in a bowling alley that had been the former Magner Hotel. It is likely that a cigarette or cigar butt from the evening's activities had ignited the combustible combination of sawdust and oil to keep the lanes greased. The fire quickly spread throughout the wood buildings, and the north side of town was soon fully engulfed in flames. Kieck's grocery store, the implement dealer, the drugstore, the bowling alley, the barbershop, the meat market and the saloon were all lost in the fire, with no opportunity to save them.

During the calamity, however, there was time for the saloon owner, Ben Johnson, to save his stock of liquor from the blaze. Johnson relocated the crates and bottles to the safety of an empty lot across the street before departing to concentrate on the fire. The stock, left unattended, survived but disappeared. It remains unclear if the stock was ransacked by those seeking to drink the liquor, prohibitionist elements or possibly both.

While a handful of opportunists were taking advantage of the chaos to help themselves to the town's supply of spirits, the majority of townsfolk sought to contain the fire. The town lacked any significant firefighting equipment, and half of the downtown was already lost. With ingenuity and limited resources, blankets, canvases and other large pieces of fabric were hung on storefronts across the street on the north side. They were repeatedly doused with water to stymie the spread of fire. Had it not been for these quick-thinking efforts, the whole town might have been lost.

By the time the embers of the ruins began to cool, work had already commenced to rebuild. A few weeks after the fire, the debris had been cleared. This time, the town would take advantage of progress, shedding the western frontier wooden front buildings in favor of sturdy brick structures. The contract to rebuild the town was award to a young but rapidly growing firm run by a pair of brickmaking siblings, and by the time the project was complete, it would be one of the first tasks for the company following the transfer of sole ownership to Peter Kiewit.

Although Papillion did avoid the physical destruction of a devastating 1908 tornado, as well as the infamous 1913 Easter Sunday Tornado that ripped through Omaha and Ralston, it has not had divine blessing to avoid all disaster. With many meticulous changes to the Papillion Creek and the establishment of dam sites, flooding has become a far more managed threat.

The 1903 flood swept through Papillion on the night of May 20 with no advance notice. The little village of Chalco, now a ghost town, was the first to feel the impact when the creek jumped its bank in the midst of heavy rains. They had tried to warn Papillion, but communication was delayed, and by then, water several feet deep had begun to rush into the streets and homes. Situated immediately next to the creek, the Papillion Roller Mills took a near direct hit, and the flour house was torn from its foundation and carried downstream. Other businesses were also subjugated to the waters. The *Papillion Times*, located in the basement of the A.W. Clarke Bank Building at this time, suffered great loses, including the back issues of its newspaper, some of which have been located since—an immeasurable loss to telling the history of Papillion in those early years. A week after the sudden flood, standing water still remained when the creek had a near repeat performance, again cresting its banks and inciting panic.

Another tragedy in the county occurred on May 12, 1908, when a tornado emerged out of a bizarrely colored sky and touched down near Richfield, where an eleven-year-old boy was killed. The funnel cloud then moved south toward Bellevue; many students from Bellevue College had gathered to watch a baseball game, while other residents went about their normal business until the skies darkened and the weather sharply changed.

The college students who could not reach the safety of a building held on to trees for dear life. The main building on campus, Clarke Hall, had its roof ripped off. Windows were shattered in other structures. In town, homes and barns, most constructed of wood, were flipped onto their sides. Debris went flying, and Bellevue resident Edward Miller was mortally wounded. The steeple of the First Presbyterian Church was ripped off and thrown into the street.

In addition to fires, floods and tornadoes, Sarpy County also encountered what has historically been referred to as a cult. Could it be Satan? Many at the time of the cult's existence held the dark lord responsible for the group's unorthodox behaviors. Known as the Figgites, they were more than merely cult. The group was deeply religious and formed because it rejected the modernity that was sweeping over Sarpy County and society.

The Figgites were started in the late 1890s in the vicinity of Gretna. At its center was Louis Figg. Like many in Sarpy County, Figg was a farmer. His eighty acres were located immediately outside Gretna. While not a literate man, his wife, Sarah, would often read the Bible to her husband. Mr. Figg grew to become very religious and increasingly opinionated, eventually believing that he was divinely blessed. Reportedly, his wife was even more radical, and she remained with him and actively supported his cause. The backbone of his gospel was complete sanctification from all that was worldly and impure. Naturally, this separation included the husbands and even children of wives who sought to join the Figgite sect. If they did not renounce marriage, they might end up in the fiery depths below. As one might imagine at the turn of the twentieth century, this situation might cause some consternation among the status quo. The breaking up of homes was not held in high regard. Furthermore, their practice of shouting, jumping up and down and behaving with the "frenzied energy of whirling Dervishes" was openly mocked.

They generated headlines with their presence, as the *Sarpy County Herald* wrote in the March 22, 1900 edition when it declared that "Forest City Citizens Go into Righteous Frenzy Over the Despicable Actions of a Gang of Fanatics Known as 'Figgites.'" The article continued, noting that if the "Figgites are crazy, they should be sent to an insane asylum. It seems the sect had a knack at luring women and mothers to leave their husbands and join the group."

It wasn't long before events became heated. A posse was formed that descended on the group under the cover of night. Words were exchanged and pistols displayed, and when it was over, the posse had forcibly removed the clothing of Mr. and Mrs. Figg before proceeding to tar and feather them. Following the incident, a report was made to the Sarpy County sheriff, who set out at all deliberate speed to track down the mask-wearing mob.

Following the attack, the Figgs had gotten the message and relocated, but not far. They moved to the relative protection of a small, isolated and generally lawless island in the middle of the Missouri River. Bellevue Island, as it was known, was home to a handful of farmers and squatters, a few moonshiners and generally people who wanted to keep a low profile. The Figgs and their followers were pursued by the law, which had determined that the quasi-lawless island between Iowa and Nebraska was actually in the jurisdiction of Sarpy County. Vigilantes might have ceased their attacks, but the ever-vigilant legal system had not. The Figgs were increasingly challenged by the former husbands of Figgites in a court of law. In July 1900, Sarah Figg was acquitted on the basis that she was insane.

By 1903, Louis and Sarah Figg were in the courtroom of the Nebraska Supreme Court. A civil suit for damages of $7,500 was leveled against them from Albert Donahoo on the grounds that his wife's affections had been alienated. The Figgs countered that Donahoo's abuse had led to the estrangement. A determination was made for a new trial in Sarpy County District Court. The battle between church and state continued but shifted the following year, when Louis Figg was jailed for refusing to send his children to school.

The island would eventually be covered with water due to flooding and changes in the path of the river. The Figgite group melted away, and Louis and Sarah Figg fell out of the public spotlight. The Figgs had seven children. All but one survived into adulthood. Sarah Figg passed away at the age of sixty-six in 1922. Her husband relocated to Omaha the last few years of his life and died at the age of eighty-five in 1933.

The Figgs and the worship of them can be considered a reactionary response to the changing times. It was more than just the addition of lightbulbs or telephones. The ripple effect of the industrial era was working its way through Sarpy County in numerous ways. Society was changing—some embraced it, and others thought it was on the verge of collapse. Either way, new challenges were faced, and often the status quo was no longer applicable. As time progressed, the frontier justice of the peace became obsolete and outdated. The model could no longer meet the demands of enforcement. Communities, including Bellevue and Papillion, shifted to the town marshal and municipal magistrate system. Springfield and Gretna, lacking a police force of their own, continued to be under the jurisdiction of the Sarpy County Sheriff's Office.

There are more than enough tales of crime, law and order in Sarpy County's annals to sustain several seasons of a long-running television drama. There are more to these true stories, however, than the hollow ones on television. On March 13, 1912, Shorty Gray, John Dowd and Charles Morley escaped from the state petitionary in Lincoln, killing the warden, deputy warden and one guard in the process. The trio of hardened criminals took off east in the midst of a blizzard and, four days later, had made their way to Sarpy County.

Grant Chase, the Sarpy County sheriff, was on the lookout for the escapees. A least six different posses of armed citizens were also formed, some including lawmen outside of their jurisdiction who sought the reward and the spotlight. Some of these officers were members of the South Omaha police force, including Chief John Briggs. Another was a police agent of the Burlington Railroad. The Cass and Lancaster County sheriffs were also in the process of gathering up and deputizing civilians.

The three convicts walked right into the Blunt homestead and demanded a farm-fresh breakfast. Blunt's wife, Carmellette, claimed that she needed to go to the chicken coop but ran for help at first chance. Insistent on eating, the convicts had breakfast before demanding that Blunt hitch up the wagon and horses to drive the convicts into Omaha, where they would very likely be able to melt away into the landscape. The quartet headed north from the farm, with a posse in pursuit. A running gun battle between the occupants of Blunt's wagon and the hodgepodge of law enforcement and armed civilians followed.

In the ensuing battle, Gray was fatally wounded; with no way out, Dowd committed suicide. Morley surrendered and was returned to prison, where he stayed until his eventual parole in 1941. He remained tightlipped about the details of the escape and potential accomplices. When the smoke cleared at the battle site just west of Gretna, the escapees had been neutralized. Unfortunately, their hostage, Roy Blunt, lay dead as well.

Held at the Springfield Opera House, an inquiry into the events of March 18, 1912, found that Blunt had been caught up in the crossfire between escapees and the posse and was fatally struck by bullets of his would-be rescuers. In all likelihood, this would have come from the South Omaha chief of police, who claimed credit for killing two of the escapees but denied shooting their captive. Sheriff Chase, who literally and figuratively came under fire, was left with a permanent limp from a bullet to the ankle during the firefight. He was also harshly criticized for indiscriminately deputizing civilians, who in retrospect should not have been granted the old-fashioned privilege.

Blunt's pregnant widow was suddenly left alone to tend the family farmstead. Roy Blunt Jr. was born five months after his father's death. The state legislature, in a move to mend the wound, voted at the governor's suggestion to allocate funds to purchase the 160-acre farm and provide a suitable university education for the child who would never know his father. Carmellette never remarried and died relatively young at age forty-nine or fifty. Roy Blunt Jr. would go to the University of Nebraska–Lincoln, marry and ultimately commit suicide at the age of twenty-six. The impact of the events of one day would have ripple effects for decades—yet another tale of history that displays the human and fragile side of Sarpy County. The Blunt tragedy can be considered the closing of Sarpy County's association with the frontier days.

Modernity brought the world closer. Between the Spanish-American War and World War I, life at Fort Crook was rather quiet. For a time, most soldiers were not even there. By March 1913, Sergeant Herman Coffman of the Quartermaster Corps had become the highest-ranking man on the post after all able-bodied men had departed for Texas to take part in the hunt for Pancho Villa. While the American soldiers that had once been at Fort Crook were unable to locate the bandit, they did allegedly gain the nickname "Doughboy" as a result of marching through the dry, dusty terrain of Mexico.

With American troops in short supply and federal troops amassed at the United States/Mexico border, the recently activated Fourth Nebraska Infantry, a National Guard volunteer unit, assumed command of the fort at the end of 1916. One of their members, Sergeant Kwan Soo Lee, was buried at the post cemetery. Sergeant Lee was a first-wave Korean immigrant who came to America in 1904. He was part of a small group of Koreans raised in Kearney, Nebraska, and was a servant for a prominent local woman. While in Kearney, he attended a military school with the intention of one day returning to Korea with his military training and experience and creating a free Korea independent of foreign entanglements. To further gain experience, he enlisted in the army in 1916 and served in the Fourth Nebraska Infantry. While on guard duty, he died in an accidental drowning death in 1917. His grave is one of the 804 interments at the now full cemetery.

Military aviation in Nebraska has its origins at Fort Omaha—not with airplanes but with balloons. These military-grade balloons were considered

Held in Springfield, the inquest into the Roy Blunt tragedy made national news. His widow, dressed in black, can be seen to the right. *Sarpy County Museum.*

vital technology to gather intelligence, monitor troop movements and serve as artillery observation posts. Between 1909 and 1921, the Fort Omaha balloon school was the largest in the world.

In 1913, the army was in a state of consolidation. The school was relocated to Fort Leavenworth in Kansas. However, just three years later in 1916, it was moved back to Fort Omaha. Europe was gripped in deadly war; the likes of which humanity had never seen before. For a time, America was a world away, deep in neutrality.

When the United States entered World War I, Fort Omaha did its part. With the increasingly visible role of aircraft in warfare and the intention of establishing a 4-million-man army, it was evident that operations at Fort Omaha would need to expand. About 119 acres about one mile north of the fort were leased to the government and dubbed "Florence Field." Here soldiers of the balloon school received their field training. By the time the school was deactivated, roughly sixteen thousand men had received training there.

By September 1918, the balloon school had outgrown Fort Omaha and nearby Florence Field. A sub-camp at Fort Crook was established to further train recruits. Upon completion of their training on November 10, 1918, they were transferred and would have begun their overseas training had the war not ended the following day. Demobilization after the Armistice was rapid, and Fort Crook once again returned to its peacetime status. Seventeen U.S. balloon companies sent to Europe saw action on the front. Of these seventeen companies, thirteen were organized at Fort Omaha. Fort Crook's first introduction to airpower through the balloon school had been brief, but its impact would last.

Sarpy County's experiences in World War I have often been forgotten, although there are a few remaining homages. The Martin-Graves American Legion Post (named in honor of Ralph Martin and Burt Graves) and the Harry Bossard and Leonard Conley American Legion Posts, representing Bellevue, Papillion and Gretna, respectively, were all named after those killed during the Great War. They were just a few of the eleven men from Sarpy County who lost their lives during the conflict. These men were seemingly an insignificant number in the scope of the roughly 116,000-plus Americans killed between 1917 and 1918. Yet they were human beings plucked from our local communities who would never return from a global war that was far removed from the rural heartland of the United States.

Harry Bossard's story might be the most tragic. Corporal Bossard was the first Sarpy County native son to die in combat during the Hundred Days Offensive in August 1918. The offensive would mark the final stage of the war, but for Bossard, it meant the end of the twenty-seven-year-old's life.

Bossard moved to Papillion in 1901 at the age of eleven. He dropped out of Papillion High School and took up jobs at the telephone company and later the electric light company. A draftee, he was called up on November 1, 1917, and was sent to Camp Funston for training. Putting his utility skills to military use, he was part of the 314th Field Signal Battalion, 355th Infantry Regiment of the 89th Infantry Division. His unit shipped out and arrived in France on June 28, 1918. Roughly six weeks later, Harry Bossard died from wounds sustained while in action. The timing of his death matches up with the unit's arrival at the front. It was the first American unit to be transported by truck to the battle lines. While relieving the unit there, they came under fire from Germany artillery containing mustard gas. It is likely that a short time later, Bossard succumbed to his wounds.

Bossard is buried at Meuse-Argonne American Cemetery in Romagne, France, Plot B, Row 38, Grave 36. The headstone at Cedar Dale is a cenotaph, a memorial headstone. Harry Bossard was outlived by his parents, two sisters and a younger brother, Royal, who served alongside Harry. He survived the war. On August 5, 1919, the newly chartered American Legion in Papillion was named in Harry Bossard's honor.

It is important to note that not all of those who made the ultimately sacrifice did so in the midst of pitched battle. Solomon Zeorian Jr. was one of these. One of seven siblings, Zeorian was born in 1894 to a prominent farm family and was raised in Springfield. He was a graduate of Springfield High School before enrolling in college at Doane. He spent two years there and then enrolled at the University of California–Los Angeles. His senior year, he transferred to Stanford University. In January 1918, he answered the call. He was serving with the U.S. Army Ambulance Corps and training at Camp Crane in Allentown, Pennsylvania, when he suddenly died after quickly becoming overcome with illness at the age of twenty-four.

The official cause of death was identified as "acute cardiac dilatation," with the secondary contributory factor as "lobar pneumonia." His family recalled that he died of a smallpox vaccination. His death might have possibly been an instance of the Spanish influenza, which was rapidly sweepingly the globe in the spring and summer of 1918. He was transported back home and is buried at Springfield Memorial Cemetery. In 1937, Memorial Auditorium was constructed at Stanford. Inside the lobby, a plaque lists all seventy-seven of the World War I Stanford fallen. The last name on this list is "S. Zeorian Jr." Between Bossard, Zeorian and the other men, each of the primary Sarpy County communities sustained direct loss as a result of the Great War—a sad occurrence that was unfortunately repeated nearly ninety years later during the War on Terror.

The First World War in the United States and in Sarpy County was a time of further change. The war meant shifting identities. That was especially true in Papillion, where there was a large number of German immigrants, who

Posing for one last photo before boarding the train to Camp Funston, the first group of men from Sarpy County left for World War I. *Sarpy County Museum.*

maintained a strong connection to the Fatherland. There was the Deutsche Platt Verein, a German fraternal organization that boasted more than five hundred attendees at its pre-picnics. The organization quickly melted away at the start of America's entry into the war. The term *German American* did not exist, and people had to decide if they were to be German or American—in a time of war, one could not be both. The loyalty of longtime community members was challenged.

There was no real pressure in pursuing American citizenship, and as such, many did not until decades after living in the United States. Such was the case of Father Henry Hoheisel, the Catholic priest at St. Columbkille. Faced with the threat of deportation by the federal authorities, it took letters of support from leading community members who could provide character statements that the good priest was not in the allegiance of Kaiser Wilhelm II. Others with less influence struggled to gain legitimacy from a suspicious government and were placed on the Alien Enemy List. Others, such as George Schram, who had started the lengthy process in September 1916, were placed on the list and remained in limbo due to the war with Germany. Schram would eventually take his citizenship oath in the summer of 1921.

While the question of loyalty remained at the time, the reality was that there was never any question of lack of commitment from those in Sarpy County. The Red Cross in Sarpy County was active during the war. Both the Gretna and Papillion chapters had more than one hundred members. A sewing circle to knit socks and sweaters met three times a week in Papillion. Funds were routinely raised for the cause. In June 1918, a Red Cross drive in Sarpy County netted nearly $15,000—the quota was only $10,000. Efforts through the Red Cross also provided knitted sweaters, surgical bandages and other supplies.

There were also financial contributions; 106 Sarpy County boys under the age of twenty-one raised $1,060 through the local YMCA fundraising drive. Whether it be patriotism or pressure, Sarpy County communities were active in war bond efforts. There were still other means of support. Organizations within Papillion's local Catholic church presented a service flag with six stars, one for each parishioner serving, and an American flag to the church to boost morale. In a more method of direct support, barrels were placed in two locations in Papillion for the purpose of collecting tobacco, which would then be donated to men in uniform.

It was not just the men in uniform. While women could not serve in the traditional sense, a woman from Gretna, Verna Snell, served abroad with the American Red Cross as a canteen worker with the American Expeditionary

Forces. A pair of sisters from La Platte also served with the Army Nurse Corps at the U.S. Army Hospital in New York.

The first to serve from Sarpy County during the Great War was one of thirty-five thousand who did not wait for the United States to formally enter. Instead, George Alden went north to Canada to enlist. Adopted by Willis and Maggie Alden, the family lived in Fairview area, south of Bellevue, before relocating to Papillion around 1900. Part of a working-class family, Alden had previously enlisted in the U.S. Army at the age of eighteen in July 1908. By 1910, he was serving at Fort Crook with Company M of the Sixteenth Infantry Regiment. It was a quiet time for the military, although Alden did deploy to the incredibly remote Fort St. Michael, in the western Alaska Territory.

When the Great War broke out, Alden, by this time a civilian, was eager to get a piece of the action. On September 23, 1914, for reasons not entirely known, he enlisted under the surname of Campbell and was officially serving with Company E, Thirteenth Battalion, better known as the Royal Highlanders of Canada, as part of the Canadian Overseas Expeditionary Force. Campbell likely would have participated in the Second Battle of Ypres in April of the following year. It was here that the Germans used chlorine gas for the first time.

Eighteen months after leaving for Canada, word came back that Campbell had been wounded in action in May 1915. He was lucky that the severity of the wound did not sideline him from the war, and Campbell continued to serve with the Canadians until June 1917. A professional soldier, Campbell would once again serve in the U.S. Army following his separation from Canada. He found himself stationed at Camp Grant, Illinois, with the 21st Company of the 161st Depot Brigade from September 5, 1918, until shortly after the Armistice, when he was discharged on November 27, 1918.

Alden/Campbell's story, while fascinating, is atypical compared to most of the World War I Sarpy County experiences. Hundreds of young men in Sarpy County registered to do their part if called on to do so. At least 269 of them drafted or enlisted. The single largest contingent of men from Sarpy County served in the 355th Infantry Regiment of the 89th Infantry Division. The unit shipped out and arrived in France on June 28, 1918.

While the boys were "over there," death arrived on the doorstep of Sarpy County. Much about the Spanish flu still remains unknown. As the world was too preoccupied with the fervor of wartime patriotism and, for many, the specter of death, the influenza often lacks in historical specifics. The origins of the sickness, for example, are not totally agreed on, as are the total dead, which ranges from 17 to 50 million and perhaps was as high as 100 million. Even with the vagueness in fatalities, what is known is that the Spanish flu remains one of the deadliest pandemics in human civilization. The grip of "the grippe" spread around the globe, including Sarpy County.

The *Papillion Times* advised the public to "avoid all gatherings of all kinds, avoid running into the disease without taking due precaution by wearing a proper gauze mask, keep in the open air as much as possible, sleep warm with all windows open but avoid drafts." Furthermore, it recommended that one "eat plenty of nourishing food, keep bowels open, and if taken sick go to bed at once and call a doctor." In addition to personal responsibility and in anticipation of the influenza sweeping over the land, the state and county acted swiftly. Schools closed, including parochial schools. Churches canceled their services. The Sarpy County Milk Producers Association postponed its meeting in Gretna originally slated for October 26. The postponement was indefinite. The foresight of those organizations to not hold public gatherings in October was superseded when the Nebraska State Board of Health issued a statewide order to prohibit all public gatherings, regardless of whether they took place indoors or outside. By their decree, schools, churches, lodges and theaters were closed until November 2. Sarpy County District Court would adjourn for several weeks, not reconvening until January 13, 1919. Further fallout included the canceling of the October wartime draft. Sixty-six Sarpy County men did not report to Camp Dodge, Iowa, between October 7 and October 11; no further men were called to duty until the all-clear sign was given.

Weddings had to be postponed or altered due to conditions. Clyde Iske and Isola Daniell were married on October 10, 1918, with only four relatives in attendance in addition to the presiding reverend. Their honeymoon was postponed until the epidemic subsided. Tragically, just a few short months later, Isola died on February 11, 1919, following an operation for appendicitis.

Postponements and cancellations likely aided in delaying the spread of the Spanish flu, but it could not prevent the first death in Sarpy County, which was reported on October 3, 1918. Typical of the era, Emily Stibal, age thirty-seven, was only referred to in the newspaper notice as Mrs. Frank Stibal. The couple resided in Gretna and together had several small children.

Of the communities within Sarpy County, Gretna would be hit the hardest. Following a succession of deaths, a strict quarantine was established. Only one person at a time was permitted to enter stores and public places. Several private homes were converted into makeshift hospitals, allowing nurses to care for the sick. By mid-November, there were sixty cases reported.

Prominent deaths from the disease included Nellie Grierson, principal of Gretna High School, and Joseph Schmitt, a local merchant. On November 12, 1918, Schmitt died eight days shy of his thirty-fourth birthday from the Spanish influenza. He left behind a wife and two young children. Grierson was not a native to Sarpy County. She was buried in her family plot in Custer County, decades before both her parents passed. Grierson was only twenty-eight.

Especially cruel, the Spanish flu was aggressive not only against those who were typically susceptible but also those who were young and normally healthy. At age twenty-six, Papillion schoolteacher Anastasia Melia succumbed to the virus. A week before her death, she had been teaching in Papillion prior to the school closure. Melia was unmarried and resided with her parents, a social normality at the time. Once home, she became ill. Her condition worsened until she was in critical condition, and then, like so many others her age in October 1918, she was gone.

The August before her death, Melia had been nominated as a nonpartisan to run for Sarpy County School superintendent, a notable feat in 1918, when women were just gaining the right to vote. Due to the prevalence of the flu, the services were held not indoors but rather in the open air at St. Patrick's Catholic Church in Gretna. The loss of a young, active and well-liked community member was a burden for her devastated parents and for those in Sarpy County.

Those in uniform were struck particularly hard by the pandemic. The threat of death was twofold. In November 1918, James Korinek, formerly of Papillion, was killed in action in France. By the end of the year, he had lost both a civilian brother and sister living in Omaha to the Spanish flu.

Gretna doctor Lester Clyde Hilsabeck spent a little under a year in uniform from October 1918 until September 1919. A first lieutenant, he served in General Hospital No. 26 at Fort Des Moines and General Hospital No. 25 at Fort Benjamin Harrison in Indiana. Hilsabeck would have been at the front lines of the Spanish flu pandemic. In October 1918, 203 of the 400 beds at the post hospital were being utilized by those stricken with influenza. Worse yet, due to the sickness, makeshift emergency accommodations had to be arranged in the hospital, in the barracks and in twenty-five tents for the 1,701 patients, of whom 1,550 were influenza cases. In the midst of the pandemic, Dr. Hilsabeck met Mary Wendling, an army nurse also stationed at Fort Benjamin Harrison. One year after the end of hostilities, they married on November 11, 1919, and together they had two children. Hilsabeck, a 1910 graduate of Creighton University College of Medicine, returned to Gretna and practiced medicine for forty-two years.

While other military installations such as Fort Benjamin Harrison or Camp Funston in Kansas were devastated by sickness and death, Fort Crook largely escaped the clutches of the Spanish flu. Early action taken by the base prevented the spread. Normally, the public was free to wander onto the grounds of Fort Crook—perhaps have a picnic lunch and watch the troops train on the parade ground. The lax attitude was suspended during the flu. Several young soldiers did succumb to the virus. Rather than be buried at the post hospital, these men were shipped home to be buried in their respective towns.

At age forty-six, Major Dr. Emil DeLanney died at Fort Des Moines. Like so many others in the medical field, he had been on the front lines of battling the flu and thus at high risk to the sickness that he would ultimately succumb to on Christmas Eve 1918. Prior to his death, he had been the medical doctor at Fort Crook and something of a notable figure in the Omaha community.

Born half a world away in Liège, Belgium, in 1873, Emil DeLanney immigrated at age six to the United States with his father. Arriving in South Omaha in 1891, he first graduated from South High School before graduating from Creighton Medical College in 1901. Almost immediately, he began a successful practice in South Omaha and served as faculty at his alma matter.

Called on to inquire if professional assistance was needed as tensions flared with Mexico, Dr. DeLanney was commissioned as a lieutenant but quickly placed into the medical reserve corps. When the Germans marched through Belgium in 1914, DeLanney took a staunch stand against the invasion. Being of Belgian descent and having spent the first six years of his life there, the attack was far more personal for DeLanney. Acting as the Belgian consul for Nebraska and the Dakotas, he became a relay to call up Belgian reservists back to their home country in the summer of 1914.

By the following year, the Belgian cause had become a lost cause, but one worth rallying around. Many Americans were outraged by the audacity of Germany in attacking a neutral nation, one that was often portrayed as a damsel in distress. In his official capacity as consul, Dr. DeLanney welcomed Madame Marie Depage to Omaha. Depage was an accomplished nurse who advocated for the modernization of nursing practices in Belgium. Her husband, a noted surgeon and head of the nation's Red Cross, remained in Europe during her American tour. The purpose of her visit was to raise money for medical needs in Europe and expose American audiences to the Belgian and Allied cause. Following her stop in Omaha in early April 1915, Depage remained in the United States for three more weeks until she boarded her ship in New York to return to Europe on May 1. Depage did not live through the voyage. Depage was one of 1,198 people, including 128 Americans, who were lost at sea when the ship was torpedoed by a German U-boat. The ship? The RMS *Lusitania*.

Two years after the Madame Depage visit, the United States finally entered the war in April 1917. Dr. DeLanney was recalled to service and appointed a major. As chief medical officer at Fort Crook, he oversaw all matters related to health and sanitation at the base. This included everything from coordinating gas mask drills to publicly warning that, for the well-being of the soldiers, women of the night must stay away from both Fort Crook and Fort Omaha. While he did have to tend to these other infectious diseases brought about by the comingling, under Dr. DeLanney's care, there was not one case of confirmed smallpox or typhoid fever between January 1917 and May 1918 at Fort Crook. When the Spanish flu began to manifest, Fort Crook was quick to enact quarantine measures and thus save lives.

After orders, DeLanney left for his ill-fated service at Fort Des Moines three months before his untimely death. Similar to the men who died of the flu at Fort Crook and were brought home, so too was Dr. DeLanney from Fort Des Moines. He was sent not to Belgium but to Forest Lawn Cemetery in Omaha. His passing did not go unnoticed. The former Fort Crook doctor's death made front-page news in the *Omaha Daily Bee*. His funeral, held in late December, was the largest military funeral conducted in Omaha for a veteran of the Great War. Officers from Fort Crook led two companies of soldiers from the base. The Fort Omaha Band and a small honorary detachment of comrades from Fort Des Moines followed, as did members of his Masonic Lodge chapter. Six medical sergeants from Fort Crook served as pallbearers. Hundreds of people lined the streets from St. Martin's Episcopal Church to the cemetery. Naturally, his wife and two children were there. All came together to honor Major Dr. Emil DeLanney. A fitting gesture for a man who gave his life upholding the Hippocratic Oath at a time when human civilization was testing its own mortality.

About 25 percent of all the deaths reported in Sarpy County in 1918 were related to the Spanish flu. Seventeen of the sixty-seven deaths that year could be connected back to the epidemic, a rather high figure considering the first fatal case did not arrive in the county until late October. Since Fort Crook was federal land, these numbers do not reflect the additional cases of servicemen who fell while serving at Fort Crook. They also don't factor in individuals with local connections (such as Dr. DeLanney) who died elsewhere and, in some instances, were buried outside the confines of Sarpy County.

While the Spanish flu is commonly associated with 1918, the calendar year had no bearing on the sickness. The spring of 1919 saw a resurgence of cases. Celia Arp, who had lived about four miles southwest of Papillion, first had the Spanish flu around Christmas the previous year. The unmarried teenage woman never quite fully recovered from the bout and, with a weakened immune system, succumbed to other complications in March 1919. Similarly, Ed Gow of Bellevue had fled to Excelsior Springs, Missouri, after surviving bout of the sickness. Excelsior Springs, akin to several other cities, was built on the qualities of nearby natural spring water, which many hoped would provide relief from tuberculosis and other disorders. The minerals were not enough for Gow, who had developed both stomach and bowel trouble following an attack of the Spanish flu the year earlier. Gow, who had been born in 1860 and grew up in Bellevue's historic log cabin, was brought back to Nebraska and buried at Bellevue Cemetery.

The Spanish influenza disappeared nearly as rapidly as it had swept through Sarpy County and the world. Its effects lingered for several years after the initial outbreak, as did a less lethal strain that occasionally continued to be fatal. For those souls who had lost loved ones from the pandemic, they would continue to feel the financial and emotional strain for years to come.

THE ROARING TWENTIES AND A NEW DEAL

Contrary to popular memory and the common historical narrative, criminal activity did not stop at the Sarpy-Douglas County border. Omaha, the big city, had its share of crime, much of it due in part to Boss Dennison, but Sarpy County was no stranger to the world of vice. By the late 1910s, the pioneer days of Sarpy County had faded away. It may not have been the big city of Omaha, but in Sarpy County, there was electricity, automobiles and county-maintained roads. These roads allowed residents to travel to church and farmers to transport their crop, as well as permitted goods and services to come and go from Sarpy County and its communities. One of those goods was alcohol, and in accordance with the Volstead Act, the Eighteenth Amendment and state law, intoxicating beverages were prohibited. Furthermore, the manufacture, sale or transport of intoxicating liquor was highly regulated to the point that it was illegal for all but a handful of uses, excluding scientific and religious purposes.

Nebraska was proactive in outlawing the sale of alcohol, not necessarily for the greater sake of progressive vision but rather driven by the belief in the correlation between sin and gin. While federal law took effect on January 1, 1919, Nebraska's first day of statewide prohibition was nearly two years prior, on May 1, 1917, although some communities had been dry in the years leading up to that. That was not true in Sarpy County, where the majority of residents had voted in favor of the new law. The man responsible for the enforcement of the law was Charlie Hutter. He may have been the Sarpy County sheriff, but Hutter's ability to carry out his sworn responsibilities was highly questionable. At twenty-four, Hutter had been the youngest person elected sheriff in the state of Nebraska when he first won his race in November 1914. In those days, the sheriff ran for reelection every two years, and Hutter continued to serve, winning two elections until he abruptly vacated the position five days into his third term in 1919. Hutter had been forced out of office on a technicality because he had failed to post an official bond as required to become sheriff. Hutter claimed that this was not negligence on his part but rather because he had been hospitalized with influenza; he blamed his attorney for not acting.

Out of a job, Hutter went to the Sarpy County Courthouse, where he demanded County Commissioner John Lilley meet him in the street. A fistfight between the two soon started. Accounts indicate that Hutter "bruised Lilley about the head," but no formal charges were filed against the former sheriff. If there were no previous indicators of the former lawman's lack of scruples, it was becoming increasingly clear to those around him. At the very least, his hotheaded temperament was now publicly well defined.

To further his troubles while battling to save his job, Hutter in 1919 received a $3,000 judgment against him for exceeding his authority by taking a man from the Sarpy County jail to the South Omaha jail. A separate suit by Mike Zweibel sought $10,000. Zweibel was the town marshal for the village of Papillion and did not take kindly to Hutter speeding through the community's streets. Hutter ignored the local lawman until Zweibel fired a warning shot into the ground. The harmless bullet caused Hutter to stop. Then, with great promptness and hostility, he arrested Marshal Zweibel, claiming that he had been the target of the shot.

In 1922, allegations of the former sheriff forging government documents were finally dismissed from a case that had been pending for the last six years. Throughout all of these activities, it has been highly speculated that Hutter continued to make a living as muscle, serving as an enforcer for noted bootlegger Tom Denison, the de facto head of the criminal underworld.

Hutter was tried on violations of liquor law with nine others in May 1928. Eight of the nine were found guilty. The one innocent man? Charlie Hutter. He apparently had been in the wrong place at the wrong time when his brother, Harry Hutter, and the other defendants had been raided by federal agents in the midst of unloading fifty-five fifty-gallon drums of grain alcohol; the raid had taken place in Papillion the wee hours of the morning and seized nearly $50,000 worth of contraband. While Hutter walked, the shipment of alcohol that had been retained by the government as evidence during the duration of the trial was poured down the sewer following the proceedings.

In January 1931, Hutter was shot in the leg. The wound was so severe that it required amputation of his left leg at the knee. Hutter claimed that it was a failed kidnaping attempt. Lightning struck twice for Hutter. In August of the same year, he was shot a second time and suffered wounds in the shoulder, arm and neck. The shooting had occurred outside his Omaha home. The former sheriff initially stated that it was the result of an attempted stickup, but no one of any authority believed it was anything other than a second attempt on his life. With his hospital room under guard by two Omaha police detectives and with a visit from the U.S. District Attorney's Office, Hutter confessed that the shootings were revenge for him refusing to give protection money to two well-known South Omaha politicians who also moonlighted by operating an illegal liquor racket. It seems that Hutter had crossed someone by refusing a payoff, and now they were trying to cross him off. Three men were arrested in connection with the shooting, and it is unknown if Hutter finally paid or if the criminal underworld, wary of the press spotlight, ultimately moved on.

Long after his tenure as sheriff and a decade after Prohibition was overturned, Hutter, ironically now the owner of a bar in South Omaha, was involved in a minor automobile accident outside the tavern. When it was over, the twenty-three-year-old driver of the other car was dead, and Hutter, age fifty-four, had driven off. He was charged with second-degree murder, and the trial ended with Hutter being acquitted due to a deadlocked jury. It remains unclear if, while serving as the sheriff of Sarpy County, Hutter was also on payroll for Denison or if this occurred following his career in law enforcement. Historically, as hindsight tends to have perfect vision, the residents of Sarpy County might have voted the wrong man into office. Either way, judging by the character and legacy of Sheriff Charlie Hutter, the enforcement of prohibition was off to a rough start in Sarpy County during those initial years.

The county sheriff did keep busy during the 1920s with frequent raids. Armed with a search warrant, Hutter's successor, Sheriff Charlie Peters, raided a pair of homes north of Bellevue in December 1920. He netted more than five hundred bottles of beer. The two men captured during the raid were ultimately given sixty to ninety days in the county jail—a relatively light sentence for the men, whose biggest worry was supposedly being locked up during Christmas but more likely would have been the income lost from the sale of their illicit homebrew. The same day as the raid, a copper still; two and a half gallons of "white mule whiskey," better known as moonshine; and several barrels of sorghum mash, used in its production, were confiscated. With all the confiscated liquor, Peters's office reportedly resembled and smelled like a bar.

These raids were frequent during the dry years. With the exception of a few instances, each case was similar. The sheriff with a warrant would raid premises, seizing contraband, and the bootlegger would be carted off to jail for his or her hearing, usually to be found guilty. One of the few cases where the sheriff arrived too late to locate any illicit homebrew was due to a bootlegger's wife, who had slipped away to dump one hundred gallons of liquor that had been stored in the chicken house. Sheriff Sam Startzer did not locate any illegal drink to confiscate, although he did have twenty-five dead chickens floating down in a foamy stream wash up at his feet.

These were not all small-time or whimsical bootlegging operations. On December 16, 1922, Sheriff Startzer raided a farm in the vicinity of Avery, north of Bellevue. The farm was not a family farm, but rather a distillery manufacturing plant, one that was large enough to possibly be operated by someone with ties to the criminal underworld in Omaha. The sheriff confiscated more than two thousand gallons of rye mash, eight copper stills, fifty-four large barrels, six gallons of the manufactured product, eight sacks of sugar, smaller kegs, flasks and bottles. The operation had been set up in the barn, basement and even an underground cavern. Transported with several trucks, the loot was taken to the courthouse, now Papillion City Hall, where it filled the second-floor hallway.

The biggest bootlegging raid in Sarpy County took place in March 1929, when the sheriff, along with both state and federal agents, broke up a significant operation, once again located in the vicinity of Avery. Nearly one thousand gallons of whiskey, allegedly testing at 90 percent alcohol, were found in charcoal-lined hardwood kegs along with one-hundred- and sixty-gallon stills at a home. The manufacturing plant even had counterfeit labels to place on bottles. It was estimated that the liquor was valued at $5,000. Those same county roads, so pivotal in the transporting of illicit alcohol, had turned against the bootleggers that spring when the heavy rains mired vehicles, especially those carrying heavy wooden barrels laden with whiskey.

The owner of the home, Percy Perry, was nowhere to be found. However, invoices, correspondence and business papers were plentiful. Perry was located one month later and went to trial at district court. He, like many others, would be found guilty, pay a fine and serve time for a crime that would eventually be repealed. Yet one has to wonder: as much as local law enforcement kept busy apprehending bootleggers, how many were *not* caught during those prohibition years? Despite the fact that alcohol was prohibited by law, it was far from unavailable; similar to the national trend, the county seemed to be awash in unregulated homebrew libations. The threat of incarceration did little to turn "wets" into "drys," as many over a decade prior had hoped.

Perhaps due in some part to the flurry of prohibition activity and the expanded role of government that coincided with the First World War, by the 1920s Sarpy County was seeking a new courthouse. Built in haste to provide a definitive end to the 1875 courthouse debate, by 1921 the courthouse was reported to be falling apart. The *Papillion Times* reported that the "Southwest Corner of the court house took a notion a few days ago to lean on the other foot a while and as a result another crevice about three inches wide was opened between the main building and the addition to the west." The emergency repair was made by installing several long iron rods to hold the fragmented building together.

What remained of the old dilapidated 1875 courthouse was sold to Hugo Cordes for $925. The top floor and cupola were disassembled, and the remaining brick structure was modified into a heated automobile garage and repair shop. The grand opening saw more than just a handful of the business community marking the occasion—rather, five hundred people were present in what was clearly the biggest happening in town that week.

As the horse and wagon continued to give way to early automobiles, meeting supply and demand, which had steadily increased during the 1920s, resulted in gasoline increasing by another 2 cents in the Papillion area by December 1925, making the price 20.25 cents per gallon. Putting that into perspective, a Ford Model T had a ten-gallon tank and reportedly averaged between thirteen and twenty-one miles per gallon.

The *Papillion Times*, critical of these high-octane horseless carriages, stated in 1927 that "some of the young sheiks of Papillion who are burning up the streets ought to be deprived of the privilege of driving a car for a few months as a wholesome lesson."

At one time, a large and visible painted sign, bearing the simple message, "Look out, cars," warned Papillion pedestrians and horse-driven buggy riders to be alert. By this time, though, the sign is no longer seen in historic photos. In 1928, the village marshal brought one speeder before a judge, where he was fined $1.00 plus court costs for a total of about $6.50 for his lead foot.

Prohibition had put a damper on the soldier's access to libations at nearby Fort Crook, but it did not reduce the activity at the base. By 1924, Fort Crook had grown in size and scope. A primitive landing field had been erected

Whether a caution against train cars or early automobiles, modernity is seen creeping into Papillion in this photo taken around Second and Jefferson Streets. *Sarpy County Museum.*

at the fort and was named Offutt Field to honor Jarvis Offutt, an Omaha military aviator killed during World War I. The dawn of aviation had come to Fort Crook and Offutt Field, which would primarily be utilized for U.S. Postal Service airmail. In the coming years, the presence and influence of airpower at Fort Crook would continue to expand.

Despite being a native to the area, it is likely that Jarvis Offutt never visited his namesake. Born in Omaha in 1894, Jarvis Offutt aspired to service in the military. Part of a wealthy and influential family, Offutt entered Yale, where he quickly realized that he preferred the chance to be a part of the new aviation section of the Signal Corps rather than the artillery. However, the aviation service of the army lacked enough planes, and Offutt received his training from the Royal Canadian Flying Corps. During World War I, Offutt was attached to the British Royal Air Force as a ferry pilot. One of Offutt's responsibilities was to deliver aircraft from British factories to bases in France. On August 13, 1918, while completing one such mission near Valheureux, France, his plane was either shot down or forced down due to mechanical error. Parachutes were uncommon for aircraft pilots at the time, and there was little Offutt was able to do. He

Jarvis Offutt, the namesake of Offutt Air Force Base, died during World War I at the age of twenty-three while flying in France. *Sarpy County Museum.*

died of his injuries and is buried in France. The Fort Crook landing field was renamed in his honor on May 10, 1924.

In the summer of 1925, the U.S. Postal Service completed a ten-plane hangar. Airmail service for Omaha and the surrounding area operated in and out of Fort Crook for the next five years. Despite the investment in infrastructure at Fort Crook, airmail service was transferred to the Omaha Municipal Airport (present-day Eppley Airfield) in 1930. The Offutt Flying Field at Fort Crook would continue to operate during the interwar period. It was an era of relative calm before the gathering storm of World War II.

Life at Fort Crook during the interwar period of the 1920s and '30s moved at a slower pace. As noted, the base found its niche with the growth of airpower. Less remembered uses during this time include its service as the headquarters for the Seventh Service Command. Eight states, as far north as North Dakota and to the southern border of Arkansas, carved out the region of the command. Each Corps Area served as an administrative district for the mobilization of manpower within the region. What appeared to be an impressive position of power was actually rather hollow, as the military between the world wars was in a rather diminished state.

In the midst of the Prohibition era, Bellevue did not entice a criminal element alone. It also attracted Catholic priests. The Mission Society of St. Columban is not one of the five formal communities in Sarpy County. However, it has its own zip code and is located in St. Columbans, Nebraska. The tiny area is landlocked by Bellevue, much the same way Swaziland is surrounded by South Africa or Vatican City is surrounded by Italy.

Despite being physically small in geographic size, the Columban Fathers have a sizeable worldwide presence and an extensive history. Their formal story began in 1918 through the efforts of Father Edward Galvin, an Irish priest who was living in the Diocese of Brooklyn. In 1916, Galvin made his first trip to China and was appalled at both the spiritual and actual poverty he encountered in the county. With the blessing of the Holy See, Galvin established the Society of St. Columban.

Originally located in the heart of Brooklyn on Bedford Avenue, the New York location was not to be permanent. At that time, Bellevue College was collapsing, and land belonging to the Presbyterian-affiliated school was purchased by the Columbans with the intention of being their new North American headquarters. There was hope for a while that the school's buildings would be acquired by the Columbans, who even placed a bid to obtain the structures, but it was not meant to be.

With a brief stopover in Omaha, Father Galvin and Father John Blowick, the order's second founder, relocated from the high-density New York City to the 215 acres of farmland in Nebraska. The town of Bellevue was described at this time as "consisting of…six buildings for a main street and a few scattered houses." Construction of their headquarters began on September 1, 1921 and was finished less than a year later in June 1922. The sparseness of Sarpy County was regarded as a positive for the Columbans, and the soft, gentle rolling hills of the landscape had an attractive quality that was appealing to farmers.

Sarpy County remained a chiefly agrarian society in the years after the Great War, and even with the consideration of prohibition-related activity, most Sarpy County residents were god-fearing farm families. One example of a Sarpy County resident would be Rasmus Foged. People like Foged flocked to the United States in the later decades of the nineteenth century and first part of the twentieth century in search of idyllic wide-open spaces with big skies to call home—places like Sarpy County. America offered a life full of better opportunities for many. Immigrants began arriving in large numbers from Europe to Sarpy County as early as the 1870s, long before Ellis Island's common use in 1892. The majority of Sarpy County's emigrants came from Germany. Many others came from Ireland, Sweden and Norway.

Taking into consideration that he was not German, Rasmus Foged's story is still an example of the immigrant experience for many who came to Sarpy County. Foged was born on December 1, 1891, in Denmark. In 1913, at the age of twenty-three, he traveled aboard the *Hellig Olav*, a large passenger ship that could accommodate between 1,089 and 1,670 passengers in varying classes. The journey from Copenhagen to New York took almost two weeks.

Most who made their way to Sarpy County did not do so directly, especially if they did not already have family here. Foged's story was no different in that sense. He first settled in Michigan before moving west with the desire to farm. That dream would have to be put on hold due to World War I. Foged, like many new American men who served during the war, were not yet naturalized citizens, but he became one while in the service. Others, in return for their enlistment, were given citizenship papers.

Following the hostilities, Foged traveled to Denmark, married and brought his wife, Johanne, back to the United States. The newlyweds rented farmland near present-day Bellevue Boulevard and began a dairy farm, Hillside Dairy, delivering milk all over Bellevue and South Omaha. By his early thirties, Foged was able to purchase 160 acres of prime farmland south of Gretna and continued farming. Together, he and Johanne raised their four children. Buried at Cedar Dale next to his wife, Rasmus Foged passed away at the age of seventy-eight on September 25, 1970. It is the individual stories of everyday residents that make up the fabric of Sarpy County and its communities. These first-generation immigrants blazed a trail for future generations, many of whom have recognizable surnames common to this area.

The Foged children and many others were involved in a budding 4-H program. "Head, Heart, Hands, and Health"—the 4-H motto was officially adopted by the easily identifiable four-leaf clover crested organization in 1927. That same year, the first 4-H chapters in Sarpy County were established. Sarpy County was still almost exclusively rural at that time. In March 1927, Packers National Bank, Nebraska Extension and the now defunct position of county superintendent of schools collaborated to give boys and girls the opportunity to compete at the state fair. The Beef Calf Club, Pig Club and Corn Club were all formed on short notice.

The response was positive, and within weeks, informational meetings and clubs had started to spring up. These typically were held in local one-room schoolhouses such as Bell and Fairview Schools. On March 31, 1927, it was reported that chapters in both Springfield and Papillion were formed, complete with the establishment of officers. In order to receive the charter, a club was required to have a minimum of five members between the ages of ten and eighteen. They were also required to meet several times throughout the year. Clubs established their own meeting times. Some met weekly and others monthly. The Fairview Girls' Sewing Club met every two weeks, taking turns at the homes of various members.

Clubs focusing on cooking, canning, sewing and even friendship were formed by the following month in April 1927. If 60 percent of the club members completed their work and filled out the related reports, they were given an Achievement Seal.

While there was guidance and support, the creation of these clubs was accomplished through volunteers, mostly teachers, and sometimes a farmer's wife. Sarpy County overcame the difficulty of organization due to the county's lack of an extension agent, an individual responsible for locally coordinating the formation of 4-H clubs and much more.

The first Sarpy County Junior Fair was held in September 1927. County clubs participated for cash prizes. The lofty loot was $2.00 for seventh through fourth place, $2.50 for third, $3.00 for second and $4.00 for a first-place prize winner. The cash prizes were sponsored both by A.W. Clarke Bank in Papillion and Packers National of South Omaha. With twenty different categories, there were plenty of participants and winners, especially because every boy or girl who had anything on exhibit would receive a prize. The one-day fair was not limited to just contests; it also featured demonstrations, 4-H reports and musical acts. Sarpy County clubs also actively participated at the state fair that year. The Canning Club hosted at Portal School submitted an exhibit, as did the Corn Club. An Aberdeen Angus calf and a Poland China female pig were entered. The calf took third place, while the pig took second in their respective categories.

Today, 4-H has a worldwide membership of 6.5 million youth. In Sarpy County, 4-H with Nebraska Extension remains strong through a number of programs and experiences that build a foundation of lifetime skills, critical thinking, problem solving and respect. In a rapidly changing world, 4-H has evolved to include healthy lifestyle choices and hands-on learning that helps youth with their futures. While Sarpy County has drastically shifted from rural to urban, 4-H has adapted to meet the needs of the community and yet continued to have a positive impact on countless local youth.

Athletics, of course, have been a large aspect of both school and local community culture throughout Sarpy County. Springfield High School had a vibrant athletic program. Football was discontinued in 1908 due to the cost and concern of injury, but there was both a boys' and girls' basketball team until 1926, when girls' basketball at Springfield was dropped due to vocal outcries that it was not "ladylike" and too strenuous for women. In Papillion, the boys' basketball team was Class G state champion in 1926, beating out more than three hundred teams from across the state. The team repeated the feat the following year. The victory celebration included a parade, dinner, speeches and wafers and punch for the whole school. A separate dinner for the team was hosted by the businessmen of Papillion.

Estella Krejci was the girls' basketball coach and principal of Papillion High School. Krejci started coaching girls' basketball in 1921. During the same year that the boys took state in the 1926 season, the Papillion girls won nine games, lost two and tied one. They outscored their opponents 380 to 207. The star of the team was forward Pearl Rothermund, a freshman who scored 221 of the 380 points that season. The March 11, 1926 *Papillion Times* headline hailed that the "Girls Close Successful Year." However, the girls, no

The Gretna girls' basketball team, seen here in 1912, was not as accomplished as Papillion's team, in part due to the lack of a gym. *Sarpy County Museum.*

matter how good they were on the court, did not have a tournament. It had been abolished by the Nebraska High School Athletic Association in 1924. By the mid- to late 1920s, girls' athletics had been squeezed out of schools throughout Sarpy County, and they would not return to for nearly fifty years until the advancement of federal civil rights law of Title IX in 1972.

With the streetcar and a few rudimentary roads, including the winding and impressive Bellevue Boulevard, Bellevue was closer to Omaha than ever before, although it still resided in the hinterland for many, similar to Boys' Town in its early years. This locale in the idyllic countryside had an exotic history rooted in the pioneer days of yesterday; it was not too far removed from the big-city bustle of Omaha and yet far enough that the pungent smell of the stockyards became distant. It was in that backdrop that Fontenelle Forest was established. Recognizing the need to preserve the untouched land, the Fontenelle Forest Association was formed in 1912. Fontenelle Forest is a natural wonder. It is also a historic district included in the National Register of Historic Places. The history of the area spans roughly ten thousand years. The woods have been occupied by native populations, a historic ferryboat crossing site and a fur trading post operated by Lucian Fontenelle. The 1,500-acre area is home to some 150 species of birds and more than thirty types of trees, including oak, walnut, cottonwood, conifer and more. The land has been untouched by horses, campers, motor vehicles, hunters and other disruptions. The serene beauty and quiet of the woods have been visited by many looking to escape the commotion of civilization and, in one instance, was the full-time dwelling of one man.

Jim Baldwin, or "Jim the Hermit," became something of a local legend within the community. He was once a clean-shaven, tough-looking young man before he retreated from society, moving into a small shanty-like home in Fontenelle Forest. Rumor has it that Baldwin suffered from the stresses of World War I—it's true that Baldwin did serve in the navy during the war. As the world outside changed, Baldwin spent decades living in the woods. Occasionally, supplies would be donated to Jim, especially as he got older. He would frequently receive visitors, many of whom sought him out to hear his tall tales. Baldwin was one of two Sarpy County hermits; the other was Henry Morris, who lived in the woods near Gretna.

Absorbed today by the woods of Fontenelle Forest, Camp Gifford provided an opportunity for urban boys to escape big-city life in Omaha and connect with the natural world. The 108-acre camp was named after prominent Omaha doctor and owner of the land Harold Gifford. In turn, Fontenelle Forest purchased the land a few years later, and an agreement was reached

Fontenelle Forest hermit Jim Baldwin is visited by Santa (Bob Roberts), Jim Roberts of KMTV and Ron and Don Gebbie in 1960. *Sarpy County Museum.*

to provide a tract of it to the Boy Scouts. The camp might have been in a rustic setting, but it contained modern amenities, including a sewer system, running water, a refrigerated kitchen, a spring-fed swimming pool, cabins and a dining hall large enough to hold 125 hungry campers.

In 1928, Scouts could attend the away camp for eleven dollars for two weeks or six dollars for a one-week session. Days were filled with swimming, boating, hikes, contests, feats of strength and numerous other scouting escapades. The most well-known legacies of Camp Gifford were the Nani-Bi Zhu tradition. One of the campers to spend several summers at Camp Gifford and be part of the elite Nani-Ba-Zhu was the future actor Henry Fonda. The ritual, shrouded in mystique, included the campers donning pseudo–Native American garb, carving totem poles and fully embracing Boy Scout oath and law. Nani-Ba Zhu and Camp Gifford remained strong throughout the 1920s and '30s, but by 1946, the camp had been given back to Fontenelle Forest. That same year, another Camp Wakonda, also on the edge of the forest, opened and continued to serve Boy Scouts for more than seventy years.

The first established scouting troop in Sarpy County, however, was in Papillion. The first official meeting for Troop No. 1 of Papillion was held on February 9, 1914, three years and one day after scouting was brought to America after originating in Great Britain. In those days, Papillion had a very small-town feel, primarily because it was a small town. The population

Bellevue resident Ed Sterba, seen sitting in this 1928 photo, was part of the Nani-Bi-Zhu program at Camp Gifford. *Sarpy County Museum.*

would have been just 630 people, yet public participation in Troop No. 1 was high that first meeting, with a reported 34 boys in attendance. Under Chief Scoutmaster and prominent Papillion attorney Gerald Collins, the troop took its first outing on May 2, 1914, a hike south of town along the Platte River. The day included fishing, boating, swimming and dinner before returning back to town. While the hike was not uphill both ways, it was a round trip of fifteen miles.

The Scouts' activities of the era included woodcraft, cooking, foraging and rudimentary military training. Memorial Day 1914 marked the first time the Scouts helped to decorate the graves of soldiers, gathering and placing wild flowers and flags at each marker. The *Papillion Times* credited their work, writing, "They will undoubtedly grow up to be brave and chivalrous men bred to defend their country if need be and to do any worthy work that demands the efforts of such well-trained boys."

Enthusiasm for the Boy Scout program continued into the 1920s. In 1921, a permanent meeting facility was erected for the Scouts. It still remains and is utilized by Boy Scouts today. Built as a community effort, the majority of the work was completed by the Scouts, while much of the materials were donated. The foundation came from the stone that had been part of the old Papillion Roller Mill. A local farmer provided the oak logs. Construction began in July 1921. Completed in November of that year, members had their inaugural meeting in the building on November 11, 1921. In 1927, the Boy Scouts organization reorganized its regional and national chapters. Papillion Troop No. 1 was renumbered and renamed Troop No. 60 and still remains highly active.

The Great Depression was a challenge for many in Sarpy County, but civilization did not break down. Nationwide, farmers had been experiencing hardship for some time prior to the Wall Street crash of 1929. Aspects of distress could be felt in more rural areas in the years leading up to cities feeling the financial pinch. For many in both the 1920s and '30s in Sarpy County, money and resources were limited.

Those difficulties are represented in education. Times were tough in Bellevue. Then came the Great Depression, and things certainly did not get much better. Student population growth was sluggish. Those who chose to attend school in Omaha were allowed to do so, with the expense to be paid for by Sarpy County. Bellevue Public Schools in 1928 had five high school teachers, and most would come in from Omaha to Bellevue in order to teach. The average salary for a Bellevue Public School teacher during the 1932–33 year was $945. The school superintendent earned nearly double that amount. This was actually better than most of the other Sarpy County public school educators and definitely an improvement in wages of those who taught in the country in rural one-room schoolhouses.

Bellevue Public Schools needed to find a solution to lacking a high school. The future of its youth was at stake. It found a solution across from the Bellevue Cemetery, where the Reed Community Center is currently located. The land the new school resided on was known as the Bellevue common area because it was a miscellaneous oddity from the days when the surveyors first made boundary lines. A hastily constructed building was built to house the students. Made of stucco, the one-story building measured forty by eighty feet. The less than glamorous roof was covered in tarpaper. For this architectural dud, the price tag was listed at $92,000. The school was formally dubbed Pioneer Union High School.

However, the building was so shoddy that the wealthier Bellevue families, who mostly lived on Bellevue Boulevard, objected that their children would be sent to school that appeared to be better suited as a sheep shed. From that day on and for nearly the next twenty years that the building served the community, the moniker of the "Sheep Shed School" remained.

The Sheep Shed School was not a permanent solution, and school officials were well aware of this by the early 1930s. Taking advantage of President Hoover's initiatives, the school in 1933 applied for $33,000 from the Federal Emergency Relief Administration, which built dams, bridges and schools all across America until replaced by the better-known Works Progress Administration. In 1936, a bond issue seeking additional funds from Bellevue residents passed in favor by a vote of 159 to 102. That same year, the school board refused admittance to military children of those living on Fort Crook unless the regular tuition was paid. It would not be until 1940, with the introduction of the Lanham Act, that the federal impact aid program would slowly make inroads in the community.

By 1937, the funds had been raised, and new high school accommodations were made. It was an addition to the original 1869 schoolhouse built at Mission Avenue and Washington Street, today Mission Middle School. Over December 1936 and January 1937, classrooms transitioned to the new building. When it was all finished, the old Sheep Shed School was sold to the American Legion for $500 following the relocation.

Federal help under President Roosevelt's alphabet soup programs did find its way to Sarpy County. The Civilian Conservation Corps spent several productive years based at Fort Crook. The Works Progress Administration (later renamed the Work Projects Administration) was active during some of the leanest years of the 1930s and provided crucial jobs to those out-of-work residents. Wage scales were based on the size of the largest town in a county. Sarpy County workers received a maximum of forty dollars monthly at thirty cents per hour for unskilled labor. That presented a disadvantage for those employed under the WPA program in Sarpy County. Since individual pay was determined by the size of the largest community, Douglas County wages were at fifty-five dollars per month at forty cents per hour. The discrepancy in pay was not lost on the men of Sarpy County participating in the WPA program. At one job site located one mile west of the Douglas-Sarpy County line, twenty-nine of the sixty workers were found sitting around with their picks and shovels when prevailing wage at that time in late 1935 was thirty-two dollars versus forty-five dollars for their neighbors to the north. Further insult occurred when projects were intended to be county-specific, utilizing local workers—that was not always the case with Sarpy County, when certain jobs required more manpower or specialized labor.

Yet there was no shortage of projects to complete. The first Sarpy County–based WPA projects started in late 1935 and would continue even through the first year of the war. Many of the small rural bridges and viaducts over streams and creeks throughout Sarpy County were built using WPA funds. The October 30, 1938 *Omaha World-Herald* reported on the $3,600 of federal government money to be used to construct one such viaduct. Some of them continue to be utilized throughout Sarpy County.

One primary aspect of WPA work was to hard-surface many of the farm-to-market roads through the use of a rock crusher and WPA labor. The burden of road improvement was taken off the county government, with its limited resources, and placed on the broader shoulders of the federal government. John Wiese, the chairman of the Sarpy County Board of Commissioners, wrote to the acting district director of the WPA based in Omaha that "it is our hope that the projects can be continued for an indefinite period, in order that every school and mail route in the county can be hard surfaced." He continued, noting that it was their "desire to co-operate in every way possible with the WPA to that end."

In the modern era, when society often demands roads to be paved and pothole free, the transition from dirt roads to gravel was a significant step in the direction of progress. An update by year's end in 1936 reported that 22,336 tons of gravel had been utilized to provide a hard surface for 36.5 miles of road. The project came at a price, but one that local city and county governments did not have to pay and in all likelihood would have been unable to afford. Wages of workers, as well as an additional $52,148 for materials, were covered by the WPA. The county's share of the price tag was far less: $13,635, or $373.56 per mile, for the benefit of never getting stuck in the mud again.

Sarpy County's quarries were further utilized for a large project in Omaha. In 1934, construction began on the American Legion Municipal Airport, and Sarpy did its part by supplying limestone for the runways from a WPA-operated quarry, where it was loaded onto train cars and taken via rail the twenty-five miles to the construction site. The airport would eventually be renamed Eppley Airfield in 1960.

This 1919 photo illustrates the deterioration of the roads. The WPA and New Deal projects assisted in graveling the dirt and sometimes muddy country roads. *Sarpy County Museum.*

Constructed between 1938 and 1940, the Springfield Community Hall utilized WPA labor to quarry sandstone from a few miles west of the town. In 1998, the hall was placed in the National Register of Historic Places. WPA funds also built county garages in each of the four towns in Sarpy County.

Thinking outside the box, Sarpy County stood to gain through the Federal Writers' Project, part of the WPA. The *Papillion Times*, the Sarpy County Historical Society and the Federal Writers' Project collaborated to print a historical booklet entitled "Old Bellevue," which chronicled the early years of Sarpy County history. The original printing consisted of six hundred copies of the thirty-two-page booklet. Printed by the *Papillion Times*, it was sold at the retail price of fifty cents per copy. The Martin-Graves American Legion post went door to door soliciting for sales of the book. There had been previous publications, but this book was the first serious initiative at gathering Sarpy County's past and telling it through the lens of community-focused public history.

A separate multi-year WPA project involved researching Sarpy County's history in greater detail. Throughout 1935 and the following year, a

As one of the most visible projects of Great Depression–era federal efforts in Sarpy County, the Springfield Community Building was completed between 1938 and 1940. *Sarpy County Museum.*

committee of seven lay people tracked down a list of 491 obituaries, 76 biographies, rosters of both active and defunct railroads, listings of county officials, lawyers, preachers, churches, banks and post offices along with their postmasters. The appointed superintendent of the local history project was a seventy-five-year-old retired Methodist preacher and active member of the newly founded Sarpy County Historical Society, Reverend W.D. Stambaugh. The historical committee members were compensated through federal funds, but their research was a passion that extended well beyond their hours of service. Furthermore, items such as a typewriter, stationery, postage and other incidentals were paid out of pocket.

Their work was made possible by a WPA grant of $3,144, but it was the community pitching in to share its history that made the project a success. Then as now, it took some serious convincing from the historical committee to get that community participation. In a letter published in the *Papillion Times*, Stambaugh wrote with frustration, citing that people tended to think that their little history amounted to nothing, yet if he arrived on their doorstep to tell them that their family history was of no consequence and amounted to nothing, he would be kicked off their property.

While the work was noble, the WPA ultimately denied their request in the fall of 1936 to support further funding in order to write an in-depth book on local history. The project was too similar to the short booklet that had previously been published through the Federal Writers' Project. Nonetheless, without their foresight and dedication during the Depression, much of our understanding of Sarpy County's past would have lost.

Community betterment extended further into education beyond literary works. The Public Works Administration—which on a national level build large-scale projects that included dams, hospitals and schools—reached into Sarpy County. Pleasant View School at Twenty-Eighth Street and Chandler Road was built with PWA assistance. The $40,000 project provided a brick-and-stone school with classrooms, a combination gymnasium and auditorium, a library and an office.

Not everyone was in favor of municipal projects that resulted in improvements to the common good. There were accusations of drunkenness on the job. These resulted in bitterness from former WPA staff and laborers who had been laid off. Additionally, those critical of the WPA's work referred to their projects as a boondoggle that was a waste of time and money. Despite the critics and the flaws, there was real positive benefit for Sarpy County. The Depression-era projects of the WPA, PWA and CCC were the first attempt to modernize Sarpy County since its inception. Between 1935 and 1939, $19 million were spent on WPA programs in Douglas and Sarpy Counties. The federal programs not only built infrastructure but also helped to inject much-needed cash into the local economies prior to the war years.

During the Great Depression, Fort Crook had housed a Civilian Conservation Corps camp. The program had been initiated by President Roosevelt to help stimulate the economy and provide steady work for unemployed, unmarried young men. Most of their work included projects within the surrounding Nebraska and western Iowa countryside. Projects such as floor reclamation, work in state parks, forestry, erosion control and soil conservation were their focus, but occasionally they were utilized to assist in construction projects on base, as was the case when the runway was enlarged to accommodate more than the old mail biplanes.

In addition to long, narrow, open-floorplan wood-framed barracks for the men of the CCC program, federal funds provided resources to build a mess hall, a motor pool, offices and a hospital annex. A preexisting building on base became the CCC "service club." The policy-driven result was that while the CCC was hosted at a military installation, the men were largely isolated from the regular army troops at Fort Crook.

Fort Crook during the interwar years was home to the Seventeenth Infantry Regiment. It held concerts, marched on the grounds and held outdated military drills. *Sarpy County Museum.*

There may have been good reason for the separation. Many of the regular army men were career soldiers, and there was a strict sense of discipline in the ranks. By comparison, CCC men were often malnourished, with only marginal training prior to their commitment of serving in the program for a minimum of six months. A difference in pay might have left a bitterness in the mouths of the soldiers of Fort Crook. In 1934, pay for a private in the army was $17.85 per month. A CCC trainee received $30.00 per month, albeit he was required to send $25.00 of that home to his family.

In 1937, while storm clouds of war were forming in Europe and Asia, in the United States a Congressional bill to modernize Fort Crook failed—either it was dramatically underfunded or those involved were indifferent or indisposed to the idea due to the hardship of the Depression. About $111,500 of the appropriations bill would have provided funding to build automotive maintenance shops and garages, modernize the telephone facilities and construct additional noncommissioned offices quarters. It was not purely a political issue for Washington, D.C. The regimental band played on, festivities and family picnics were part of base life at Fort Crook and parade ground review of the troops continued to be emphasized in army life. Photos from this time feature members of the primitive campaign hat–adorned Seventeenth Infantry Regiment at Fort Crook utilizing wagons and hooved animals rather than trucks and jeeps. Neutrality, not war, was America's aim, but that would soon change.

CALL TO ARMS

Sarpy County and World War II

Fort Crook would find itself tasked with the crucial mission of building the arsenal of democracy by supplying the Allied war effort during the Second World War. By late 1940, it appeared that the United States would eventually get involved. In January 1941, the Martin Company of Baltimore leased a large portion of Fort Crook from the U.S. government. The company's bomber plant in Baltimore near the East Coast was considered vulnerable to German attack. A bomber plant on the West Coast would be vulnerable to Japanese attack. A location in the middle of the country seemed safest.

The hospital, six units of officers' quarters, the NCO Club, Post Headquarters, Band Quarters, the Civilian Conservation Corps Camp and golf course all disappeared as giant bulldozers moved more than 5 million cubic yards of dirt to level the land to build the Martin Bomber Plant and a new runway. Storehouses and extra tents were filled with supplies for the new construction.

The construction of the plant was quite a feat. By the numbers, it was staggering: 250 miles of electrical wiring installed; forty-seven thousand cubic yards of concrete poured; 10 million square feet of paint applied; five acres of glass installed; and 10 miles of fluorescent lighting installed. With a total floor space of 1.2 million square feet, twenty-five football fields could have fit into the facility.

With the enormous size and scope of the project, construction operations took place around the clock, hardly pausing when the United States officially

The *Martin Star* served as the company magazine for employees and featured their efforts as well as the plant life at Fort Crook. *Sarpy County Museum.*

entered the war. Less than one month following the attack on Pearl Harbor, the bomber plant became operational on January 1, 1942.

The main facility of the bomber plant is known as "Building D." Thousands of B-26 Marauder and B-29 Superfortress Bombers, including the *Enola Gay* and *Bockscar*, the planes that would drop the atomic bombs on Japan, were built at Fort Crook. Japanese surrender and the war's end would come not long after. Operations wound down rather quickly following Japan's surrender, although production continued until the final B-29 rolled off the assembly line on September 18, 1945. Dismantling of wartime machinery came quickly after that, and the once bustling production facility fell silent. Total production of bombers numbered at 2,116; 1,585 B-26 Marauders and 531 B-29 Superfortresses were assembled at the plant. A further number of B-24s, B-25s, B-26s and P-40s were reconfigured at the modification plant.

The Martin Bomber Plant at Fort Crook has a special distinction. Of all the aircraft production facilities in the United States, the Martin Bomber Plant in Nebraska was one of the best. With thirty-three consecutive months of on-schedule production, no other facility even came close to meeting its efficiency expectations.

That record can be credited to the hard work and dedication of the workers at the plant. Requests were featured in newspapers such as the *Omaha World-Herald* for workers, and they eagerly responded. Many were young local men and women, excited by the opportunity to join the ranks of the large production facility. Others were from across the Midwest, brought to Nebraska by the prospect of steady employment after years of living through the Great Depression. By the final year of the war, the Martin Bomber Plant of Nebraska employed 13,217 individuals. The majority of those, 11,019, worked in the main facility. Another 2,198 workers were employed in the modification center, overhauling existing planes to increase their effectiveness. More than 40 percent, 5,306, were women; 765 were African Americans. All contributed to the war effort.

Frequently omitted from popular memory, wartime Fort Crook was more than home to the Martin Bomber facility. The base was active during the war serving as a training facility for mechanized training, providing classes for GIs to keep an army of trucks, jeeps, halftracks and other vehicles rolling along. When the automotive maintenance school was discontinued in April 1945, the school had a capacity of 2,100 students per session. A total of 21,000 enlisted men and another 3,000 officers had graduated. Among the graduates were two classes of civilian women. The first and

Harold Hall (*far right*) and other employees in October 1945, standing beside the last of 531 B-29 bombers to be completed at the plant. *Sarpy County Museum.*

more successful of the two had 142 of the 150 initial enrollees graduate from the three-month program in April 1943. Additional graduates included a detachment from the forces of the Free French, as well as 40 Italians who had sworn allegiance to the United States and were being trained for noncombatant duty.

The base also housed prisoners of war from the Axis forces. Historically, many Germans worked the fields of Sarpy County. They were immigrants who came to this country as far back as the 1850s in the search of opportunity, and they found it as Nebraska farmers. The Germans captured on the North African and Italian battlefields during World War II did not arrive in Sarpy County in identical circumstances. They were sent to Nebraska during the war to help local farmers in their fields due to the wartime manpower shortage. The help was appreciated, and relations between Nebraskans and the captives were generally good.

Perhaps the two groups could find commonalities between them. That seems to differ from the relationship between Italian prisoners of war, about 150 to 200 of whom were held at Fort Crook and who, outside of a few anecdotes, have largely been forgotten about. More than 250,000 Italians surrendered to Allied troops in the deserts of North Africa. By September 1943, the fascist government of Benito Mussolini had capitulated, and what was left was entirely a puppet state of the Nazis. While the war raged on, the Italians remained in custody of the United States.

Those who found their way to Fort Crook in January 1944 found themselves being put to work locally, most either at an army laundry facility or a cold storage plant in Omaha. They would be paid at the price set by the Geneva Convention, receiving eighty cents per day in the form of canteen coupons. Additionally, they were allowed two pints of beer per day. Their knowledge of English was extremely limited, and reports indicated in a rather foreign tone that they consumed mass amounts of spaghetti in cooking oil rather than butter.

In November 1944, those working in the laundry facility refused to go to work. Unhappy with their jobs, they were put on a restricted diet in response. It was only a few days of this punishment before the strike was broken and the Italians were back on the job. In May 1945, a much smaller work protest occurred when fifteen Italian prisoners went on strike. The strike only lasted two days on bread and water rations before the prisoners returned to work.

Sixty-five Italian POWs had already organized a "sit down strike" at the Omaha Cold Storage company facility. A full investigation took place, and both the army and the United Packinghouse Workers of America Union could not figure out what the prisoners' grievances were. Beyond the surface, the issue was much more threatening to the war effort. The labor union was no advocate of the Italian prisoners and had already protested the presence of the prisoners. In fact, it voted unanimously that if the Italian prisoners were not removed from employment at the plant, Local 120 would go on strike. UPWA representatives declared, "They had better use enough to man the entire plant because their union members would not work with them."

The company had the authorization for the sixty-five prisoners to work in the plant and had asked for an additional thirty-five Italians, but that request was delayed until tensions subsided. It seems that they finally did when the military backed down rather than risk a significant worker strike from the union, which was already unhappy with the wage freeze in place since the start of the war. The certification was pulled for Italian POWs to work at the cold storage facility, and they quietly were sent to help in other ways as the war's end drew ever nearer and the American public's attention begin to shift to postwar life and postwar pay. In the year after VJ day, more than 5 million Americans would go on a wave of labor-related strikes.

A great effort was spent on activities related to Fort Crook, particularly the Martin Bomber Plant, and it is an incredible story that involves not only a local connection but also national and international history. As previously mentioned, the plant and military installation retooled for the war effort at breakneck speed, but what of Bellevue, the community directly adjacent?

Strategic Air Command ensured that Bellevue and Sarpy County would remain viable several years after the Second World War ended, but it was the construction of the Martin Bomber Plant that served as the spark to transform Bellevue and Sarpy County into what it is today. In 1940, Bellevue was a hamlet with 306 residential dwellings and a population of 1,184 to fill those structures. Rather than backward, the community was quaint and rural, typical of many small towns throughout the state. There were no streetlights or signs, sidewalks, sewers or paved streets, and there was no real reason for there to be. Instead, there was quiet, fresh air and no hustle and bustle or big-city problems like in Omaha. However, with the dawn of war and the coming of a major wartime facility, Bellevue had no option but to change its ways.

In 1941, the village acted quickly and decisively. Initial steps were taken. The first step, for those who were savvy and financially able to do so, was to buy all the land. Bellevue's pioneer days were filled with hopes and dreams, most of which never came to fruition. However, the village had been organized with more than four thousand lots, most of which were empty, but they would not be for long with the prospect of new homes and businesses to keep a small army of airplane factory workers sustained.

A public land sale took place in January 1941. The land's 1,300 lots had been delinquent from unpaid taxes for several years, and as such, Sarpy County was now going to sell them. Despite the speculation of land values rising due to the major construction project, the individual lots did not sell for much, averaging only fifteen dollars per lot, with many of them going for as low as three dollars.

In his *Nebraska History* journal article "Public Leadership in a World War II Boom Town: Bellevue, Nebraska," Jerold Simmons stated that this occurred for several reasons, including poor public notice of the sale and restriction to the number of bidders, but the greatest impact stemmed from the mutual understanding between Bellevue residents that driving the price up for the lots in a bidding war would only hurt profits and would not be beneficial to any of the more established citizens when the influx of new residents arrived to town with the hope of finding a place to live. Another tactic by this same bidding bloc was to encourage the auctioneer to only sell entire blocks rather than specific lots, thus restricting the property ownership to specifically those who could afford a sizeable amount of land, as well as those with the means to develop the empty lots into neighborhoods. This initial auction manipulation would only continue for so long, and in subsequent county auctions, the price of lots continued to rise steadily.

The homes that would be built on these lots were the equivalent of houses built for workers of the Hoover Dam nearly a decade prior in Boulder City. The Bellevue homes were affordable, no-frills homes that would be eagerly purchased by those seeking to live minutes from their jobs at the bomber plant. The homes could be purchased from $3,750 to $4,250, and required only a small down payment of a few hundred dollars was required. Ray Jungers, a bomber plant employee, paid $100 down and $27.29 per month for his Bellevue wartime home.

Many of those who purchased homes, including Jungers would continue to live in Bellevue after the war ended. Others saw themselves as temporary workers, and while rates on homes were affordable, these bomber plant employees sought housing that could be more transitory in nature. The Glenn L. Martin Company contributed $1,620 for the construction of a trailer park to help the housing shortage for workers who did not have the means or interest to have a little pillbox home that one day would be their own.

Housing developers came in all sizes in the development of Bellevue. At one extreme, nearly two hundred homes were built by local landowner and beer distributer George Rushart, the founder of the Rushart Building Company. Rushart's addition covers a sizeable chunk of Olde Town Bellevue, from Lincoln Road to the east side of Calhoun Street extending south to Twenty-Third Street and the Columban Fathers Mission. Of course, there were smaller enterprises. Not letting his part-time mayoral position get in the way of the housing boom, Mayor Freeman built fifty homes. Most of the construction was limited to those with Bellevue and Sarpy County connections, although a few builders from Lincoln joined in the scramble. One of them, E.C. Westcott, would build the first attempt of a twentieth-century downtown with the construction of Jack Nester's Super Market on Franklin Street.

With the building of structures well on its way, an overhaul to the inadequate or absent infrastructure was needed. The next step was for the small town to rely on big government. Taking advantage of FDR's alphabet soup programs, Bellevue leaders applied for $130,000 in federal funding through the Works Progress Administration to cover the costs of a major sewer overhaul, allowing the construction of thirteen new miles of sewer lines and disposal plant to serve a community of four thousand. They followed up their April submission with a July request to the Public Works Administration for $360,000 to fund a new potable water system with wells, pumps and an iron removal facility. It also included construction of twelve miles of water mains. A further request that same month was sent to the Public Works Administration for a health center in the form of a grant and a loan to cover the local expenses for work to be completed on the WPA sewer project.

The school districts that served Bellevue were antiquated and sought federal assistance too. Bellevue Public Schools asked for $375,000 for a new elementary school and to add an addition to the high school, one of several that would take place through the years on present-day Mission Middle School. Rural School District 5, which served parts of Bellevue Boulevard and the Avery area that would eventually be annexed by Bellevue, gained $200,000 for its own projects. Both of these grants would be awarded through the Public Works Administration.

Simmons pointed out that this successive streak of federally funded projects to improve the quality of life in Bellevue was ambitious, and it may have led to an overconfidence when officials continued to request assistance. Three weeks shy of Pearl Harbor, the City of Bellevue approved a grant for a new police station with a jail, a city hall, a library, an auditorium and a recreation center. The city might have approved the proposal, but the Public Works Administration did not. That said, with dogged effort, the city eventually did receive federal funds in 1944 to build a police and fire station. In May 1940, 280 individuals signed a petition to retain Walter Havenridge as village marshal. However, his days were numbered, and by 1943, the modern Bellevue Police Department had been established, with Frank Maxey serving as its first chief of police. With these changes being made, the city streets were never properly addressed, despite all the growth, and this became a source of consternation for the better part of the next decade.

Much of this rapid boom began to narrow quickly as materials and resources were shifted over from civilian economic boosting efforts and retooled to help the war effort. The Federal Housing Administration, which provided loans to builders, found that it had to shift its resources for other national projects, and allocations became far more stringent for Bellevue. By that time, plant workers were finding homes throughout the Omaha metro; it is important to remember that while Bellevue had a surge of population and construction, the majority of bomber plant workers still came from nearby Omaha or Council Bluffs.

Bellevue, indeed all the towns in Sarpy County, did its part during World War II. The Sarpy County homefront during the war had the trimmings of the same great patriotic fervor that swept the nation. In 1942, Henry Doorly, publisher of the *Omaha World-Herald*, led the charge for a statewide scrap metal competition. All of Nebraska's ninety-three counties participated.

In Sarpy County, each town had a scrap chairman responsible for overseeing the collected metal from his respective communities. Almost nothing was sacred, and nearly everything that could be collected was. Plows, stoves, bumpers or even entire vehicles were collected for the war effort. The *Papillion Times* goaded readers into contributing, less they risk reading their name in the paper under the headline, "Sarpy County Citizen Refuses to Help Win the War by Keeping His Scrap."

The intimidation may have worked, as the following week, when the final tally was in for the three-week-long scrap drive, Sarpy County placed an impressive ninth place statewide with a total of 1,962,696 pounds, or 181.14 pounds of scrap per resident. The war effort in Sarpy County wasn't just limited to a three-week stint. A second surge of activity took place in the fall of 1942, when a scrap drive competition set state against state.

A county-wide scrap day was scheduled for Tuesday, October 20, 1942. The mayors of Bellevue, Gretna, Papillion and Springfield, as well as all three county commissioners, signed a proclamation that work at farms and businesses be suspended for the day. Schools spent the day not on reading, writing or arithmetic but rather focused on the scrap drive. In addition, the courthouse offices were also closed to the public, and employees were encouraged to locate scrap. This was not a ceremonial proclamation.

It was recorded that the personnel of practically every business, professional office, courthouse office and tavern donned overalls and supported the scrap gathering efforts. The one-day efforts netted Sarpy County another three hundred tons of scrap. This was metal that would be turned into everything from helmets and machine guns to B-26 bombers produced at the Martin Bomber Plant at Fort Crook.

Despite an impressive run, Sarpy County did not win the content. Its 10,835 residents supplied the war effort during both the local summer and national drives with 307.02 pounds of scrap per person, more per capita than Douglas and sixty-six other counties. Of the ninety-three counties, Hooker County with its 1,253 residents yielded the most, with 995.80 pounds of scrap per person. However, it was actually Grant County that won the $1,000 war bond for providing the most scrap during the summer drive. As a side note, the 19,178 residents of Richardson County served as the biggest loser, only supplying the war effort with 77.86 pounds of scrap per individual.

On a national level, Nebraska was the sixth-highest contributor of scrap metal during World War II, a homefront feat given the spare population of our state compared to many of the other great forty-eight. While Nebraskans remember the efforts of the Martin Bomber Plant, North Platte Canteen or munitions factories, the state also proved its worth during the Second World War.

The people of Sarpy County further did their bit by growing victory gardens. By March 1942, 818 families in Sarpy County had enrolled in the Victory Home and Garden Program. Sarpy County was able to can a combined 42,102 quarts of fruits and vegetables, which was valued at an estimate of nearly $18,000. The Keep 'em Rolling 4-H club of Sarpy County taught its fifteen boys to operate and repair tractors, a useful skill that bridged both farm and military training, as the teenage boys were eager to use their mechanics training in the navy.

In addition to the scrap drives and victory gardens, there were personal contributions. Lorene Bennett was born in Bellevue to farmers Harry and Elizabeth. After graduating from Bellevue High School, Lorene got off the farm and attended the University of Nebraska. In June 1943, Lorene wed Lawrence Chandler at the old Bellevue Presbyterian Church. Lawrence was an ensign in the navy and was stationed in Washington, D.C. A wartime bride, Lorene joined her husband in D.C. five months after the wedding.

A few months after arriving in Washington, D.C., Lorene had settled into her new life. Her husband was working in the code breaking division of Naval Intelligence. She found work supporting the war effort at the Bureau of Standards lab, conducting experiments to create a new type of aviation fuel—a commodity hard to come by. However, just two weeks after her work began, on March 5, 1944, a horrible accident occurred in the lab. An explosion hurled her through the second-story window. In addition to her injuries sustained from the fall, she was severely burned. One lab worker broke his leg, while three others were also burned. Lorene passed away a few days later. A civilian casualty of the war effort, one who has largely fallen through the cracks, Lorene Bennett Chandler was laid to rest at Bellevue Cemetery.

By D-day, more than seven hundred men and women from Sarpy County were serving in the military. There are dozens of tales of courage from the heartland, including that of Don Lienemann of Papillion. As Lienemann served with the 100th Bomb Group as a B-17 navigator in the skies of Europe, his bomber was shot down by German fighters during a raid on Ruhland Oil Refinery on September 11, 1944. The results of the mission were considered good despite the fact that twelve bombers and one hundred crew were lost on the mission. Of the nine men aboard the *Now An Then*, only three survived, including Lienemann, bailing out. For Lienemann, the war was over. He would spend the next seven and a half months as a prisoner of the Third Reich at Stalag Luft I until it was liberated by the Soviet army in the final days of the war.

Another Papillion airman, Willard Horn, joined the military one month and one day following the attack on Pearl Harbor. After extensive training, which he excelled at, Horn found himself copiloting a B-24 at one of the most remote spots in the Pacific Theater, Munda Airfield in the Solomon Islands. There were wild tales and several close calls, including once instance when the plane limped back home and was able to land with a damaged nose wheel and without instrumentation and brakes, narrowly avoiding skidding off the edge of the runway and into the ocean below. The plane never flew again. The crew survived, credited with shooting down six Japanese Zeros.

Horn continued to face death when, in the spring of 1944, the B-24 he was piloting was attacked by a lone Japanese Zero. Within sixty seconds, it was over. Smoke filled the B-24. Most of the men were already dead from being strafed by the enemy fighter. Others did not bail out in time, their fate sealed. The Japanese plane continued, making a few extra passes on the few parachutes that filled the sky. Of the twelve aboard the B-24, only Horn and another man, both wounded, made it below to the shark-infested waters of the Pacific.

The Greatest Generation: Willard Horn of Papillion was one of more than eight hundred men and women from Sarpy County to serve during World War II. *Sarpy County Museum.*

The B-24 companion plane to Horn's was able to drop a raft and supplies and radio their approximate position before leaving them to their fate. The pair found themselves in a small, yellow inflatable dingy in the middle of nowhere. They floated for four days and three nights before the two wounded men were pulled from the ocean by a friendly aircraft.

Following this narrow brush with death, Horn returned stateside and continued his career as a flight instructor. Willard Horn flew seventy-five combat missions and was the recipient of the Distinguished Flying Cross, Air Medal with seven Oak Leaf Clusters and the Purple Heart.

There are countless other individual narratives of veterans from Sarpy County and its communities. Most had the good fortune of being able to return home, but at least twenty-three men with strong ties to Sarpy County lost their lives while in uniform during the war. They served and died in every theater of operation—in Europe, North Africa, stateside and the Pacific. However, just like with the losses from the Civil War, World War I or the conflicts that have taken place since World War II, there is no Gold Star memorial honor roll in the county to collectively display their names and highlight their sacrifices.

World War II serves as a pivot point for American history, and the story of Sarpy County mirrors that grand narrative. The county emerged with the potential to be a superpower in the state of Nebraska. It was stronger and more influential, ready and optimistic to meet the postwar challenges ahead. Life would continue for those living on the plains of Nebraska—it would just look and sound different during the modern jet age.

POSTWAR BOOM

The last B-29 rolled off the assembly line on September 19, 1945. More than fourteen thousand employees received their final paychecks. The machines and equipment were removed. Building D, the main aircraft assembly plant, stood empty. It was designated as a "standby building," mothballed but kept in basic repair as part of the postwar industrial reserve program. The other major buildings of the Glenn L. Martin—Nebraska campus and Buildings A, B and C—were occupied in June 1946 by various units, including the 4,131st Army Air Force Base Unit, which maintained administrative oversight of the base.

During this time, Offutt Field's primary function was to serve as the Reserve Training Headquarters for twelve Midwest states stretching from Illinois to Wyoming. As of December 31, 1947, there were thirty-four assigned aircraft at Offutt Field, the majority of which were trainer aircraft. Personnel consisted of a total of 71 officers, 674 enlisted men and 340 civil service employees. It was during these years, sandwiched between the fervor of World War II and the heightened alertness of the Cold War, that Offutt nearly receded back to its 1930s interwar sleepiness. A far cry from the bustling days of World War II, Offutt might have been just another military installation decommissioned since the cessation of wartime hostiles had it not been for the footprint of the facilities built by the Glenn L. Martin company.

As American airpower entered a new chapter, so did Fort Crook when the recently minted U.S. Air Force and new occupants of the old army fort christened it "Offutt Air Force Base" on January 13, 1948. That same year, Offutt would serve as host base to Strategic Air Command, the overseers of the United States' strategic nuclear arsenal. The decision to relocate Strategic Air Command to Offutt from Andrews Air Force Base was not an automatic one. It was selected from forty sites, and elected officials and the Omaha Chamber of Commerce had to solidly compete for the honor. With the use of fifty trucks and a C-54, the move took ninety days to relocate from Maryland to Nebraska.

The story of SAC at Offutt would not be complete without General Curtis LeMay, who actually had nothing to do with the decision to relocate to Offutt. He had been preoccupied with the Berlin Air Lift when Offutt was selected, but there was no question that he would be the man to run SAC. Led by the leadership of General LeMay, the capabilities of SAC became greatly enhanced. In 1948, when he assumed command, SAC had 51,965 military and civilian personnel under its command.

For the first decade of SAC's existence, security through global airpower was not based in an underground facility with state-of-the-art technology but rather in a building that originally lacked air conditioning. At a cost of $375,000, air conditioning had been installed in October 1949. Retrofitting the Martin-Nebraska facilities was commonplace and often piecemeal. The original runway built for B-26s and B-29s fresh off the assembly line increasingly saw limitations in the jet age of the Cold War. In 1955, the runway was extended an additional 4,700 feet. The work to extend the runway resulted in the 183-acre pit that would eventually become the base lake recreational area. With dignitaries on hand from Omaha and Bellevue and in the presence of General LeMay, a B-47, a backbone of SAC's bomber fleet, was selected to be the first plane to utilize the updated runway.

By 1957, the same year LeMay handed over the reins of leadership, he was appointed the vice-chief of the air force, relinquishing his command of SAC to his very capable protégé, General Thomas S. Power. LeMay had built an air force empire, and Power had inherited SAC with personnel numbering more than 224,000. While many of them were stretched across the globe, it was Offutt Air Force Base that was the heart and brain of SAC. To meet the influx of personnel and dependents, new housing and dormitories were constructed at Offutt. SAC itself began its tenure at Offutt, operating out of a medium-size office building. It was a holdover from the Martin Bomber facility. That original building still stands and today is used by the Fifty-Fifth Wing Law Center. In 1957, Building 500, a state-of-the-art facility, was completed and occupied by SAC. Constructed at a cost of $9 million, the

President Kennedy visited Offutt once as a candidate, seen here with Generals LeMay and Power, and then later following the Cuban Missile Crisis. *Sarpy County Museum.*

three-story building also descended several stories below ground, allowing for spacious room to house the large maps and charts required to keep tabs on the United States' strategic nuclear capabilities.

To support all of these units and their operations, Building D nearly became its own sustainable city. A grid system, much like the city planning of Chicago or New York, was created to minimize the number of lost souls meandering through the massive building. The north–south hallways were given numeric listings, while the east–west hallways were assigned phonetic designations. Filling Building D was a post office on the top floor, a barbershop on the lower level, a base printing plant, a publication distribution office and the 55th Avionics Maintenance Squadron's precision measurement equipment laboratory. Other tenant units included the 544th Intelligence Exploitation Squadron, the 1,000th Satellite Operations Group and the 3,428th Technical Training Squadron to provide on-site training to officer, enlisted and civilian members of the intelligence community. Building D also housed a bowling alley, three tennis courts and wood hobby shop. Finally, in case of attack, Building D doubled as a civil defense shelter. Throughout the Cold War, Building D and the original Glenn L. Martin facilities continued to serve an active and diverse role at Offutt Air Force Base.

The old fort had embraced the new Cold War identity through both new and existing buildings. A number of these, such as the Cold War–era barracks, have since been demolished. Others were damaged in the 2019 flood of the base. Their future remains unknown. One building continues to sparkle in the sunlight: the SAC Memorial Chapel. Built in 1956, the SAC Memorial Chapel's most unique feature is its striking twelve-by-fifteen-foot stained-glass memorial window. The idea for this one-of-a-kind window was conceived in 1958 by SAC Commander General Power to remember the sacrifice from those SAC personnel who had lost their lives while serving their country. Following a successful fundraiser campaign, the memorial and other symbolic windows were unveiled on May 29, 1960, and the chapel was designated the SAC Memorial Chapel. The nondenominational chapel highlights faith, service and hope, accompanied by the grim undertones of global nuclear warfare.

When World War II ended, so too did the civilian jobs at the Martin Bomber Plant at Fort Crook. Within a few short months, many of the wartime Rosie the Riveters were back to being full-time dutiful wives and homemakers. Boyfriends and husbands returned from their duration of service. Families were started. In Bellevue, there had been a housing boom of nearly five hundred new homes before and during the war to accommodate the plant workers. Lured by the affordable housing, families decided to either stay in Bellevue or relocate from Omaha.

On December 7, 1945, four years to the day after Pearl Harbor, volume one, issue one of the *Bellevue Press* was printed. It was the first public newspaper for the Bellevue since the 1860s and much needed in the growing community. Its editor, John Gebbie Jr., was a twenty-nine-year-old army captain. His father, John Gebbie Sr., served as the paper's publisher and business manager. The new paper was endorsed by Bellevue mayor S.J. Flowers, who provided the first editorial, writing that the war had brought about rapid but unbalanced growth. Now with war over, Bellevue could catch up on its infrastructure, and "with the help of everyone Bellevue can be made into one of the most beautiful suburbs in this section of the country."

Those early newspapers indicated a mix of uncertainty about Bellevue future. One article compared Bellevue to ancient Rome. Whereas Nero fiddled while Rome burned, would the postwar residents of Bellevue be Nero's stepchildren, doing nothing while their community withered away? There was certainly credibility to this position, some of which was out of the hands of local residents and municipal leadership. Bellevue Public Schools, for example, had heavily relied on federal aid assistance during the war. But in time for the 1946–47 school year, the district found that its war-inflated dependency on federal dollars had ceased, and with it came a shortfall of $30,000.

Others were less philosophical, more interested in what would become of the hulking but now empty bomber plant. The Omaha Chamber of Commerce remained positive that the facility could be converted for manufacturing, perhaps even partitioned for two different companies. While there may have been activity behind the scenes, the wartime buildings remained vacant during these uncertain years.

There was also hope and optimism. No one was quite certain what the identity of Bellevue would look like, but the postwar potential was not lost on community leaders and civic organizations, such as the Lion's Club and American Legion, both of which were considering constructing buildings for their organizations. Between the advertisements for Bellevue Hardware, Brooke's Café, the Squeeze-Inn, Freeman Real Estate and an annual subscription of two dollars per year, the newspaper offered a concerted voice that Bellevue would not be just another war town, left in the lurch with the return to normalcy. Rather, Bellevue would be the architype of prosperity and stability in postwar America.

Make no mistake, however, the years between 1945 and Strategic Air Command's arrival in 1948 cannot be taken for granted. It was not until the arrival of Strategic Air Command that Bellevue's stability was firmly entrenched. While the future of Fort Crook and the Martin Bomber Plant remained in question, residents of Bellevue busied themselves with meeting the demands of a modern, progressive community.

Minor but important items included updating the city code so that all future construction of buildings would adhere to modern standards such as fireproofing and plumbing conventions. This was regulated by the creation of the Bellevue Planning Commission. While the regulation brought an extra layer of government, it also brought with it structural safety and provided much-needed revenue when the city and schools found much of their wartime federal assistance gone. In 1947, building permits totaled $621,350, with the majority of that coming from new residencies, as well as $80,000 from the construction of St. Mary's new parish school. As a side note, the land for the new school had been donated by home builder George Rushart, who had built two hundred homes at the very start of the war. While new residential and smaller new commercial construction was occurring, the Bellevue Business Association collaborated with city leaders to assist in recruiting outside businesses and helped to control the narrative

Home builder George Rushart, newspaperman John Gebbie and his dog, Skeeter. Behind them are steel frames intended for two hundred Bellevue homes in this 1947 photo. *Sarpy County Museum.*

in an effort to promote that the city was open for business as the population was nearing five thousand.

The efforts to modernize the city streetscapes and construction projects and entice development paid off when on March 15, 1946, it was announced that Bellevue would be getting a new power plant. The Loup River Power District would employ forty to fifty workers for the plant once the $9 million project was completed. While the project would take about two years to finish, it was a major accomplishment for Bellevue during these uncertain years. The power plant was made possible through the desire to establish public power districts rather than create a corporate-owned utility. Involved in that 1933 initiative, Harold Kramer of Columbus devoted his professional life to providing power to the people of Nebraska. Unfortunately, the Bellevue power plant would be one his last projects. Kramer passed away at the age of fifty-six in April 1949. The new facility would be named Kramer Power Plant in his honor.

The coal fired plant was used until 1987. A symbol of onetime progress, by then it was outdated and inefficient. It then sat dormant for another fifteen-plus years until its demolition in 2003. The land was turned into a park, and it was briefly renamed Kramer Park before being renamed the more nonspecific American Heroes Park. At present, the only remaining aspect of the past and this once mighty symbol of Bellevue's progress is a small portion of the power plant that hugged the river.

With continued success and a growing population, Bellevue still found itself geographically isolated. If one wanted to enter or leave Bellevue and head east, there were a few options, the two nearest being the South Omaha Veterans Bridge or the narrow toll bridge in Plattsmouth. Admittedly, neither of these options to cross the Missouri River was very far, but they were also not conveniently located in town.

The Bellevue Bridge was promoted as a great way to avoid the big-city traffic of Omaha if one wanted to head east. There was always a toll to cross the 1,975-foot bridge, the first of which was paid on December 9, 1952. The only problem was that while Bellevue had carved itself into a modern 1950s metropolis, there was little on the Iowa side of the river, including roads.

The transformation to modernity did not always come via the path of least resistance. For years during the late 1940s and early 1950s, there had been an effort to pave Bellevue's streets, but there had always been community pushback. There were those who felt that paved roads were unnecessary as a whole. Others objected to the associated costs and perceived the bells and whistles such as surface coatings unnecessary.

The height of Bellevue's progress was celebrated with a two-day event on September 19–20, 1954. The "Festival of Progress" was, of course, was an opportunity to showcase and celebrate the modernity of Bellevue, but it also served as an homage to its historical roots. On Sunday, following the grand parade, which of course proceeded after church, the reinterment of Chief Big Elk took place at Bellevue Cemetery.

After his death in 1846, Big Elk was buried on a high hill that would later become known as Elk Hill. In 1883, development of Bellevue College spurred the decision by officials to relocate the grave, which was determined to be in the way of progress. At the time, there would have still been Native Americans and pioneers alike who would have been alive to remember the chief. It was decided to move him just a short distance away in front of the college's main building, Clarke Hall. Apparently, to ensure that he was never alone, Big Elk was buried with fifteen other tribesmen. Their intentions would have been thoughtful at the time but would be far from respectful today.

Following his removal from Elk Hill, the remains of Big Elk unceremoniously sat in a box at city hall until 1954, when he was finally laid to rest at Bellevue Cemetery. Fundraising by the Sarpy County Historical Society allowed for a proper headstone to be installed. More than one thousand people attended the rededication, which was led by members of the Omaha Tribe.

Monday, September 20, 1954, was declared a holiday by Mayor Joe Morgan for all between the ages of 5 and 105. Actor Robert Francis, star of *The Caine Mutiny*, was in town to promote his newest film and sign autographs, but the real headliner was Vice President Richard Nixon. The vice president toured Offutt Air Force Base before a visit to Bellevue. Two hundred other federal, state and local officials were expected to attend, with Nixon providing an address during the official dedication of the Bellevue Bridge. Nixon's comments were brief and largely focused on freedom. He also reminded those in attendance that he was from a small town himself before the Bellevue school band played him off; he immediately left for Omaha to deliver remarks to Douglas County Republicans.

A ribbon-cutting followed the vice president's remarks, and subsequently, political leaders had a few words to say as well. Both the governors of Iowa and Nebraska were advertised as coming. Neither was there, but the

The Bellevue Bridge, with toll operator Ben Houghtaling. Bellevue resident Rube Ballard was the first to officially cross the bridge. *Sarpy County Museum.*

Bellevue reveled in its postwar progress. This large billboard bridges the community's history while featuring its modern accomplishments. *Sarpy County Museum.*

ladies of the Grand Army of the Republic were there to cut the ribbon. The bridge further linked two of the richest agricultural areas in the world and provided another crossing between the eastern and western halves of the United States.

The 1940s and '50s were not all prosperity. Drifting further from the modern American memory was the threat of polio. The mere mention of the disease at one time could create an atmosphere of uneasiness and fear. It is difficult for those who were not around prior to Jonas Salk's vaccine breakthrough in 1952 to imagine a world with polio, but it was very real and very near at hand. Just ask anyone old enough to remember, or quite possibly you can recall the family member, classmate or neighbor down the street who had been diagnosed with the debilitating and even life-threatening disease. Even after Salk's discovery, it took another three years before the test phase was completed and the vaccine made available to the public. Sixty years later, there are still hundreds of cases today in parts of Africa and Asia. Prior to science dominating the sickness, the polio epidemic was widespread in the United States, including right here in Sarpy County.

Founded by Charles S. Reed, the Bank of Bellevue marked the first time since the pioneer days that the town had a bank. *Sarpy County Museum.*

In the late 1940s and early 1950s, both the *Bellevue Press* and the *Papillion Times* were filled with stories of those who had fallen ill to the sickness or continuous campaigns in conjunction with the March of Dimes to help raise funds at the local level to fight this national epidemic. It was announced in February 1953 that $7,330.05 had been raised by the community, excluding Offutt, for the March of Dimes. The funds raised came about from a variety of ways and means. Collections were taken up at school. Farmers went door to door. Carnivals were held. The Mothers on the March, another door-to-door campaign, netted more than $2,000 across the county for the cause. Area money raised from the local drives would be paired with national funds to help pay for medical expenses of victims, but it was rarely enough. That same year, there were a reported thirty-five thousand nationwide cases of polio.

The 1954 campaign exceeded the anticipated quota and previous year's total, bringing in $7,725.17. When combined with the total from a separately counted Offutt AFB, the final number reached $13,580.02 toward the 1954 March of Dimes campaign to eradicate polio. Despite funds raised, there was still no official method to combat the disease beyond experimental testing. That would soon change.

In April 1955, the county raised $12,756.40 through the March of Dimes to help distribute the vaccine to all first and second graders, who had been signed up by their parents. Other grade levels would have to wait until a later date. Inoculation centers sprang up throughout the county in larger districts such as Bellevue, in Papillion Public Schools and in the numerous small rural school districts. Local area doctors administered shots to a reported 918 countywide first and second graders; there were a few tears, but at a rate of three vaccines administered per minute, most children had little time to react before it was over. The policy of inoculation was bold but not radical. Similar immunization efforts had been sponsored by public schools and Parent Teacher Associations in cooperation with the Sarpy County Health Department to inoculate against diphtheria, whooping cough, tetanus and smallpox.

By the summer of 1955, the disease that had previously spared no one, including the wheelchair-bound president, Franklin Roosevelt, had suddenly been vigorously suppressed. Yet polio hadn't been defeated. In August 1955, there were eleven county-wide polio cases reported, ranging from age one to twenty-six. However, with Salk's vaccine in hand, the number of polio cases in Sarpy County and the United States began to dwindle rapidly. Further vaccine efforts continued by Salk and others, and it wasn't long before the iron lung, metal braces and wheelchairs were replaced with the prospects of a brighter future.

Summertime in Nebraska can be oppressive. Each summer, polio would spread its wings. Public pools would close, and before air conditioning was commonplace, there were few places to beat the heat. The movie theater has typically been at the top of the list of summer escapes. For a nickel, one could sit in the cool dark and enjoy a film. During the Great Depression and before the war, there might have been time to see a film in Sarpy County but little money to do so. Given the postwar prosperity, there was both ample leisure time and addition financial means for many to enjoy that time to the fullest. There was also additional capital to construct movie theaters in Sarpy County.

In 1948, Bellevue gained a movie theater, a welcome improvement from the occasional showing of pictures in the high school gymnasium or religious films at local churches. Theater owner Byron Hopkins's debut film was *Down to Earth*, starring Rita Hayworth, plus a pair of animated color cartoons. When the lights first dimmed and the projector started whirring, the theater did not have a formal name. A public contest was held, and the name Elk Theater was chosen. The name had been submitted by Ted Bender and

Waldo Shallcross and was a nod to Bellevue's historic Elk Hill. The name did not stick and would eventually be changed to the Belle Theater.

The same year, in 1948, the new Papio Theater brought amenities to the residents of Papillion. The four-hundred-seat theater was described as having light pastel interiors, a pair of modern projectors in fireproof booths, bathrooms, a cry room for unruly children, a theater office, a mandatory concession stand and, of course, air conditioning. The *Papillion Times* stated that the addition of the theater would help "make Papillion the trading and entertainment center of the county." The manager and owner of the theater, Art Sunde, was set to host the grand opening on July 29, 1948.

The theater did not open that last Thursday in July. Parts for the air conditioner did not arrive and delayed the whole operation. Additionally, the concrete sidewalks had yet to be poured, and the installation of a canopy overhang had been delayed. Despite these setbacks, the theater had a second shot at its grand opening on August 5, and this time, 250 attendees were in for a treat. For the prescreening event, the film *Carnival in Costa Rica*, along with an accompanying cartoon, was the first film to flicker through the theater's projectors.

The next night, the Technicolor film *I Wonder Who's Kissing Her Now*, starring June Haver and Mark Stevens, was the regular feature. Admission was fourteen cents for children and forty cents for adults. It wasn't long before a full schedule of films was available at the Papio. Unlike the multiplex theaters of today, where a film can remain at the theater for weeks or more, most pictures were only run for audiences for just a few showings. During opening week that summer, there was a Laurel and Hardy film on Friday and Saturday; the Sunday, Monday and Tuesday show was *That Hagen Girl*, starring Ronald Reagan and Shirley Temple, as well as the critically panned film *April Showers*.

Films continued at the Papio for more than three full decades, although it occasionally shut down due to the recurring floods that plagued downtown Papillion when the Papio Creek jumped its banks. This was the case during the 1964 flood, when several rows of sandbags were placed at the doors to stem the tide of water flowing into the theater's lobby.

In the summer of 1981, the First Baptist Church began using the theater for its services until the congregation's auditorium was completed. Following the sermon, the building would then be switched back to theater mode. That summer, Indiana Jones battled Nazis for control of the Ark of the Covenant. By then, movie theater market share had diminished with direct-to-video, numerous cable television stations and premium channels like Showtime

Built in 1948, the Papio Theater provided air-conditioned entertainment. It also was an indicator that postwar prosperity had arrived in Papillion. *Sarpy County Museum.*

and HBO. The expenses of operating a theater were up and profit margins narrow. The larger chain theaters had rapidly replaced the independent owner-operators.

For more than thirty years, the Papio Theater provided entertainment to Papillion. Movie magic at the Papio created memories for countless children, for the baby boomers who saw many a western or for the Generation Xers who watched multiple screenings of 1977's *Star Wars* as part of their childhood. For many who experienced movie going there, the Papio Theater holds treasured memories of a past time in Papillion.

Rio Bravo—starring John Wayne, Dean Martin and Ricky Nelson—had just finished playing its run at the Papio Theater. Down the road, a new community with little history but plenty of ambition was seeking to make a name for itself. "La Vista Seeks Status as Incorporated Town" read the headline of the poorly aging *Papillion Times* on February 18, 1960. About 190 individuals of the small community signed a petition to ensure that the roots, all 335 building lots of their fledgling village, would grow into a city. There were predictions that the new community would become the second-largest city in Nebraska within a period of two years. That same week, La Vista schools, operating under the auspices of the Papillion School District, hired its third teacher. A Papillion resident, the new teacher was brought in to corral the fifty-three students, from kindergarteners through fifth graders. That number would increase to sixty the following week and only continue to rise.

With the establishment of La Vista, the new community become something of a burden on Papillion schools, which now were mandated to provide an education, yet the infant city lacked the tax base to pay for schools. For three years, several small cottages accommodated the K-5 population of La Vista. By 1963, Papillion School District was looking for a way out and filed a lawsuit with the hope severing ties with La Vista. Despite the district's disinterest, voters approved an $800,000 bond the same year to build G. Stanley Hall and La Vista West Elementary. The year after, Omaha, which had been looking to invade across county lines, sought to swallow Papillion schools in the consolidation race and bring them under the tutelage of Omaha Public Schools. Voters of La Vista and Papillion came together to vote down the initiative. Despite the collaboration, it would not be until 1987 that La Vista was made a partner and added to the school district's name.

This April 1963 photo displays the future site of La Vista West Elementary. *From left to right*: Linda Mansfield, Janet Hinkle and her sister, Kathy Hinkle. *Sarpy County Museum.*

La Vista is not in a bubble. There were mixed reactions to its creation. Most of those in Papillion were cautiously optimistic to the new city but concerned regarding operations of schools, fire department, streets, zoning and several other municipal aspects. The City of Omaha was not so agreeable. Its planning director was quoted as saying that "they would want to resist any attempts to block the future growth of Omaha." An effort to annex Omaha across county line was looming in the not-too-distant future, but at this time, it was only mere sabre rattling from the giant to the north.

The Sarpy County commissioners gave their blessing for the new community, and the appointed city trustees met soon after until an election could be held. Between the short stretch of appointees to those democratically elected representatives, the first baby born to be born in La Vista took place on March 12, 1960, at 7108 Gertrude Street. Just like a newborn itself, the new community was very young. The single polling location for La Vista residents to elect their five city council members was at a private residence, 7346 South Sixty-Ninth Street. The original ballot was blank because the town had not been in existence long enough for caucuses to be held. With no names formally making it on the ballot, everyone was a write-in. As can be expected, it led to minor chaos, with 61 different names appearing on 249 ballots. Residency requirements were also waived due to the recent incorporation.

At the same time, La Vista sought to double, expanding its size another eighty acres and 336 lots. The Papillion Volunteer Fire Department was looking to discontinue service to the area because it was expected that the new town would look after itself by either establishing its own firefighting force or signing a separate contract. Thus, the La Vista Volunteer Fire Department was born out of necessity.

All of this action took place between February and April 1960. By the end of April, the population was 1,360, roughly half that of Papillion and nearly double the size of Gretna. As seen in a window of just three months, the acceleration was rapid. There was no playbook, no guide to build a modern city. The town had numerous hurdles to clear in the weeks and months ahead. The first-generation pioneer La Vista residents were less interested in documenting their legacy and more focused in their efforts in the pride and sometimes struggle of building their modern city on the prairie.

In 1962, homeownership was not a wild dream but rather an obtainable goal. The Sweetheart model home was advertised to include all the amenities and creature comforts of modern living: gas heat, gas range, forty-gallon water heater, three bedrooms, hardwood floors, a full basement and more than twenty feet of closet space. Water, gas, sewer lines and sidewalks were in place and all paid for. The down payment cost for such splendor? A mere $99.50, and no down payment was needed at all for those eligible for GI financing.

Prices were competitive. A new community in Sarpy County was emerging out of the cornfield. The House of Nines, sold at the catchy price of $9,999, could be bought for a down payment of $99. These are remembered as being some of the first homes to purchase for those seeking to live in new La Vista. There were soon other options; for $81 per month, the steep-roofed Alpine-style three-bedroom home was an option. For the family seeking a little something more, the Colonial bi-level offered four bedrooms and even a double compartment kitchen sink for a monthly payment of $110. These options and others offered by homebuilder Decker Enterprises ranged between $9,300 and $15,600.

The possibility of moving to the remote land of Sarpy County was not all that remote for those seeking an alternative to the hustle and bustle of busy Omaha. The lure of green lawns, driveways, sidewalks and wide streets brightly lit at night and modern homes and schools was often convincing enough. Model homes were available for a walkthrough for those who needed any extra encouragement.

The designer colors to suit a consumer's individual taste were not the only reason why homes were being built. The desire to move near the big city while avoiding its pitfalls brought scores to Sarpy County. The population doubled from 1950 to 1960 and then doubled again between the following decades. Jobs were being created both in Omaha and in Sarpy County. Housing stock was needed at a rapid rate. Even with the employment opportunities of the Martin Bomber Plant, the population in Sarpy County in 1950 was 15,693. By 1970, that number had swelled to more than 63,000 residents calling Sarpy County home.

Many of these 1950s and '60s homes are still well lived in and well loved. A few retain their original looks. The majority of homes have been altered over the years with vinyl siding, additions or nuanced changes in their appearance to give each home individuality. It has been argued that these houses might outlive their more recently built counterparts, although following the collapse of Decker Enterprises and subsequent inquiry, the 1968 U.S. Congressional Record referred to La Vista as an "instant slum" in part due to shabby housing. On the other hand, better and more durable materials have given way to larger lots and houses with dozens of customizable features. The improved quality of housing has helped Sarpy County maintain a tremendous rate of growth.

Through all the progress, new homes, polio epidemics and amusements, there was communism. Not in any actual form, but rather the mere perception and anxiety that a Red Menace might infiltrate Nebraska. Perhaps it would come to Sarpy County and infiltrate the organizations the community held dear.

The Columban Fathers have had several encounters with greater historical events. While based in Bellevue, they soon found themselves in the midst of civil war in China. Several priests were rounded up and held in captivity for three months—one died shortly after his release, and another was outright murdered.

The Chinese civil war was interrupted by the Second World War when the Japanese invaded in 1937. Six priests of the Columbans were killed during that conflict by the Japanese while completing missionary work in the Philippines. When the world war subsided and the civil war in China resumed, the Communists by then had gained the upper hand. After this victory in 1949, Catholic priests and any other Western religious influences were forcibly expelled. In 1952, influential priest Edward Galvin left the country. By 1954, all 146 priests belonging to the Columban Society had been ejected from Communist China.

The 1955 film *The Left Hand of God*, starring Humphrey Bogart, is a significantly Hollywoodized story of a Catholic priest within the backdrop of the Chinese civil war, perhaps utilizing the Columbans in China as basis for the highly fictionalized story. For many of the Columbans, the reality was much crueler.

Following expulsion, Galvin did not return to Nebraska; ground down in both health and spirit, he went to the land of his birth, Ireland. He died there in 1956, but half a world away, Galvin Road, christened after Galvin's death, continues to bear his name, a testament to his lasting impact on Bellevue.

Beginning in 1955, it was illegal for a citizen of the Soviet Union to visit Sarpy County. The U.S. government feared that Soviet intelligence agents might be too free to roam about the country. Additional concerns were held about everyday Soviet citizens, who upon returning home might be interviewed by communist press agencies that would publish the travelers' criticisms of the American way of life.

Soviet citizens were permitted to visit some 70 percent of American territory, including Omaha and most cities with populations greater than 100,000. Americans, likewise, had similar rights when visiting the Soviet Union. The general ban was lifted by President Kennedy in 1962, but restrictions remained for Soviet reporters and government officials until the end of the Cold War.

Between the Red Scare, only further drummed up through McCarthyism, and the Cuban Missile Crisis, bomb shelters were being dug in a handful of instances in Sarpy County. There is at least one shelter in a residence in Papillion that was toured by local 4-H members. Another anecdotal story holds that a Gretna farmer built his shelter with a window, so he could see the mushroom cloud envelop Offutt Air Force Base. There was no harm in trying, but many were aware that should something dreadful occur, Sarpy County, with its connection to Offutt, would have little time to worry about anything if the civil defense sirens were to sound.

General Power oversaw SAC during some very tense years during the Cold War, including thirteen days in October 1962 when the risk of the United States and the Soviet Union entering full-scale nuclear warfare over missions in Cuba was at its apex. Peace, not war, was the profession of SAC. SAC oversaw not just bombers but also in-flight refueling tankers, strategic reconnaissance and even missiles. However, it was the command and control, the nerve center of SAC, that was at Offutt. The safety of that command and control could not be guaranteed should Offutt fall victim to a direct hit. Additional measures had to be taken, dubbed the Looking Glass Operations.

For twenty-four hours a day, seven days a week, 365 days a year for twenty-nine years, the Looking Glass at Offutt remained constantly on alert; from 1961 until 1990, an EC-135 was airborne, serving as command center in the event of a full-scale nuclear war against the Soviet Union. In a gloomy post-attack scenario where command and control was obliterated on the ground, operations would still be able to continue.

In the meantime, there was still much to be done on the ground and at home in the Sarpy County communities. Local PTA groups often screened films such as the Cold War classic *Bert the Turtle*. Civil Defense informational programs were held, and speakers were invited to chat on a variety of topics as they related to the Soviet Union, Communist China and other subjects connected to the Red Menace.

Alice Weeth was a mainstay for public education in Sarpy County. She began her teaching in Gretna in 1913 and served as an elementary school teacher for the next forty-two years, until her retirement in 1955. As was the case with many women who devoted their professional lives to teaching, Weeth never married, but she did teach generations of Sarpy County residents how to read.

District 32 directly served Springfield. Despite the relative static population growth of the community, to meet the demand of student population, new schools were built in 1876, 1884 and finally 1918, when the all-brick Vintage Building was constructed. In addition to reading, writing and arithmetic, high school classes were held for typewriting; manual training, which was all boys; and domestic science, which of course was all girls. In the decade after World War II, these subjects might have continued to remain mainstays, but there was so much more activity taking place both in and out of the class at Sarpy County's schools.

Throughout the 1950s, the longtime educators of Bertha Barber's and Alice Weeth's era were retiring. Safeguarding children against the ills of communism was not what they had been taught at two-year teacher college some four or five decades prior. Changes, reform and a redirection of focus related to education were taking place. In 1958, a major overhaul for Sarpy County education occurred when thirteen rural school districts and Springfield formed a new consolidated district. The result was Springfield Platteview Community Schools, which covers an overwhelming 93 of Sarpy County's 248 square miles. The fabric of Sarpy County was becoming more closely stitched together and, with it, continued to shed its rural upbringing.

NOT JUST FLYOVER COUNTRY

By the 1960s, the post office had modernized. Zip codes went into effect on July 1, 1963. Papillion had outgrown its storefront post office. A new freestanding building was in the works, and the public was invited out for the dedication; coffee and donuts were to be served. Dignitaries including Congressman Glenn Cunningham and Senator Roman Hruska were going to be in attendance. A full page in the *Papillion Times* was devoted to promoting the event. The time for the dedication was scheduled for 2:30 p.m. and the day November 22, 1963. It never happened. Instead, just two hours earlier, at 12:30 p.m., President John F. Kennedy was assassinated in Dallas. Today, that building is the current postal facility that serves Papillion and La Vista, and if you're waiting in line, which can often be the case, you might notice a dedication plaque hanging near the counter to mark the post office's dedication and the death of the president.

In 1968, John F. Kennedy's brother, Robert Kennedy, was campaigning his way through the country as candidate for president. One month before his own untimely death, Bobby Kennedy visited Sarpy County, stopping at the new Southroads Mall and speaking to crowds of people, hoping especially to rally the potential youth vote. The 500,000-square-foot mall had opened two years prior to Kennedy's visit. In its heyday, the mall had two hundred stores, with anchor stores being J.C. Penney, Woolworth's, Sears and Brandeis, the last of which eventually became a Younkers.

New malls such as Westroads and Mall of the Bluffs opened, drawing people away from the Bellevue mall. The real death knell to Southroads

Taken in October 1965, postmaster John Munnelly of Omaha with a Kennedy plaque. The Papillion Chamber of Commerce and public donations helped to defray the cost. *Sarpy County Museum.*

was the "Kennedy Curse," the opening of the JFK Freeway, which allowed motorists to simply bypass the once primary north–south connecting road to and from Bellevue and Omaha. By the early 2000s, little activity remained at the once mighty mall outside of mall walkers seeking exercise and John's Grecian Delight, a small but popular restaurant with a die-hard following. There have since been several nontraditional attempts to breathe life into the dead mall, but for many of a certain age, going to Southroads Mall was an important cultural part of growing up in the area.

Besides the initial commercial success of Southroads Mall's opening in 1966, the year was also a landmark one for higher education in Sarpy County with the opening of Bellevue College, a dream of local entrepreneur Bill Brooks. He pushed for support through the Bellevue Chamber of Commerce at an annual meeting. Those in attendance fully supported the project. After nine months of studies and surveys, a plan was formed and carried out by a five-member board of directors, consisting of Brooks, Hugh Campbell of Bank of Bellevue, John Reinhart, L.A. Campbell and Harold Smock.

The college did not want to imitate other institutions, full of young college coeds; rather, by design, Bellevue College focuses its efforts on the nontraditional students—night school attendees, military personnel looking to gain credit hours and those already in the workforce who sought higher education. With tuition roughly $1,200 per year compared to $1,500 to $1,800 at University of Nebraska, the price was more attractive for working people and those managing life's challenges.

After the planners created a four-year college out of thin air, the first classes were due to start in the fall semester of 1967 with ten faculty members and an initial class of four hundred freshman. By the end of the first four years, it was believed that the school would have an eighty-acre campus with fourteen buildings, all of which would come through private financing rather than a publicly funded university reliant on taxpayer dollars. True to the focus of the nontraditional student, Brooks was part of the first graduating class. His academic career had disrupted by World War II, with Brooks serving as a Marine Corps aviator, piloting the under-gunned *Brewster Buffalo* at the Battle of Midway before returning home. He maintained several successful businesses, notably a popular gas station, but never got back on track to finishing his final year of school until Bellevue College.

Ten years after opening, the little college that had begun in a World War II surplus Quonset hut earned full accreditation and offered twenty-one areas of study, with degrees granted in fourteen majors. A gem to tout was the college's library, which contained forty-five thousand volumes and another ninety thousand documents in its ethnographic collection, which included more than three thousand cultures. It would not be until 1994 that Bellevue College became Bellevue University.

During the 1966 inaugural year for Southroads Mall and Bellevue College, a debate was taking place in the courtroom of the Nebraska State Supreme Court. In the twenty years since the end of World War II, progress in Sarpy County had been moving along at a steady clip. The result was a greater population and more industrial and retail outlets than ever before, and this attracted the attention of the city of Omaha. What was of interest to Omaha was not its history but rather its expanding tax base and future potential. The courts decided that the city of Omaha could not annex territory in a foreign county, a move that ensured that Sarpy County would not be swallowed up by the big fish, as had been the case for South Omaha, Millard and Elkhorn, once independent communities with their own municipal governments and respective histories. The decision ensured that each of the respective cities in Sarpy County would continue to develop at its own rate of growth, including both the fledgling La Vista and Papillion, which was just on the cusp of looking over the hill where the city had crested since its 1870s railroad days.

By the 1960s, Papillion had only just begun to think beyond its nineteenth-century boundaries. The natural progression of development and increasing number of paved roads, along with the backdrop of a pair of devastating floods, provided cause to expand Papillion out of the reach of the Papillion Creek.

Papillion had time to dry out in the years that followed the 1903 flood, but several smaller floods did take place. It was only a matter of time until the next great flood occurred. That took place on August 2, 1959, and was declared worse than the waters that had run their course through Papillion in 1903. This time, evacuations did occur, but once again basements and first floors were not spared. Papillion had modernized with the rest of society, and as such, the impact of the floods increased. Whereas the mill had been lost fifty-six years earlier, this time around there was perhaps more at stake. The bridge over Washington Street shifted and settled twelve feet in half an hour. The bridge became impassible, and with it, the north and south sides of Papillion were cut in two. Worse yet, the rains continued, and after several days, the water stretched from present-day Papillion Middle School all the way to the center of the Washington Street between First and Second Streets.

Streets signs are being put in place in Papillion by Harold Ely (*left*) and William Lindner (*right*). *Sarpy County Museum.*

The title of "worst flood" was scooped up a few years later and awarded to the 1964 flood. The water continued to rise, causing nearly $5 million in damages, with $2.8 million of that assessed for urban areas. Similar to the 1903 floods, the rapid rise of waters prevented evacuations, causing several people to nearly drown, including two individuals who clung desperately to a tree branch until being rescued. Elsewhere, the flooding of the Papillion Creek was blamed for seven deaths. Being the only county in Nebraska surrounded by water on three sides, with the Papillion Creek jutting through the interior of the county, is a wonder, but one with a potentially dangerous outcome unless suitably harnessed.

Moving away from the original boundaries of Papillion, the development of Tara Plaza would serve as a major catalyst in the evolution of Papillion. Where corn once grew, the shopping center would provide a bridge between Papillion and the community of La Vista, itself established only several years prior. The sleek, modern shopping center provided a competitive alternative to downtown Papillion. Construction took place over the spring and summer of 1968. The grand opening took place on August 31, 1968. Congressman Glenn Cunningham, several county commissioners, the mayor of Papillion and the commander of Offutt Air Force Base were several of the dignitaries present. At the center of the ribbon cutting and development was Mike Hogan.

A born and raised Papillion resident, the twenty-seven-year-old Hogan developed his first homes in Papillion in 1956. A few years later, in 1960, he developed the 450-area home known as Tara Heights. Over the years,

Beardmore Chevrolet sustained damage from the flood of 1964. Other autos were hastily moved out of harm's way by anyone able to see over the wheel. *Sarpy County Museum.*

several other homes, apartments and commercial properties would be built under his leadership. As he was proud of his Irish heritage, many of Hogan's developments or the nearby streets would have connections to the Emerald Isle. At thirty-eight years old, while serving his third term on the Papillion City Council, Hogan was there to cut the green ribbon at Tara Plaza. He would make the plaza his nerve center, relocating his offices there at the time of the grand opening. Hogan passed away in 2016 at the age of eighty-seven after developing and managing many more Sarpy County properties.

The original retail of Tara Plaza included the five-thousand-square-foot Ben Franklin as an anchor store. Upon its debut, Ben Franklin was part of the largest group of variety stores in the nation, with more than 2,400 franchise locations. Guitars, shoes, televisions, ironing boards and more were all part of the Papillion location's inaugural sale. While franchise stores still can be found on a national level, the Ben Franklin Company filed for bankruptcy in the 1990s.

IGA Green Hills Supermarket also quickly moved into the plaza. One of five stores in the Omaha metro area, Green Hills was brightly lit and boasted the lowest prices and the finest service. The grocery market is notoriously competitive, and over the years, the store changed ownership several times. By 1983, there were three other grocery stores operating within two miles of Tara Plaza, including the Hinky Dinky and the Bakers in Brentwood Plaza.

Lynam Drug, Cabby Lounge and Package Liquor, Flowerland, La Neice Coiffure Beauty Salon and Kirby Rogers, Attorneys at Law, were all original tenants. Max I. Walker, the then fifty-one-year-old business, opened its twenty-fifth store at Tara Plaza.

With recent sprawl and commercial havens such as Shadow Lake, as well as the impact of the online realm, Tara Plaza has faced considerable competition in recent years. That said, with a busy gym and favorites like Ming's and Grecian Gyros, Tara Plaza still attracts visitors fifty years after it first made its mark on Papillion in 1968.

The year 1968 was one of development, but growing pains went along with that change. Neighborhoods grew out of fields, and the physical makeup of what they looked like and who often lived there was changing too. Memories and history are often linked. Usually they have overlapping qualities, but often how we remember things and the actual historical sequence of events that took place can have notable differences. More than fifty years later, America remembers the civil rights work of Dr. Martin Luther King Jr. That memory has become one of unilateral unity against ignorance and bigotry, highlighted through marble statues, postage stamps, essay contests

Modernity came to Papillion in the 1960s through ribbon cuttings and paved roads. The bridge through downtown had an opening ceremony in 1961. *Sarpy County Museum.*

and volunteerism. King's death, and subsequent events emanating from it, resulted in people responding to the situation with a variety of mind-sets. This was also seen in the local response in Sarpy County. This response highlights just how King's efforts and legacy were met with a mixed reception at the time of his death in April 1968.

In a number of America's major cities, grief turned to violence. Chicago, Baltimore, Kansas City and dozens of other communities saw major riots. Cities burned. Five decades later, some areas have still not recovered. April 7, 1968, was declared a national day of mourning. In Bellevue, the city complied with LBJ's presidential proclamation that flags would be lowered to half-staff in honor of Dr. King. However, at least one local resident and reportedly several others during this time of official mourning stopped by city hall multiple times to raise the flag back to full staff. Others made phone calls to city hall. It was also reported that one person even removed the flag. Respect for Dr. King was not unanimous.

The end result was a decision made by city officials to simply have no flag at all. Mayor Robert Haworth was "disgusted by the whole thing." He said that "if the city couldn't show a little respect without having a guard at the

Concrete is spread in November 1963 along Washington Street as a new sidewalk takes form in Papillion's business district before Tara Plaza. *Sarpy County Museum.*

flagpole from morning till night," then the solution would be to "avoid the problem by having no flag."

Not everyone agreed with this approach. Norm Magnusson, city council president and later county commissioner, said that while he "couldn't fully agree with all that Dr. King stood for," this was a presidential proclamation and the city government of Bellevue should uphold that decree and not succumb to pressure so easily. Magnusson added that police protection of the flag should have been utilized and that anyone caught tampering with the flag should have been arrested.

Father Robert Garvey of St. Mary's Church vocally supported Dr. King and was outraged by the events at city hall. He was inclined to write a letter to the editor to the *Bellevue Press*. Garvey was aghast that this would happen in his community. He expounded on the basic lack of respect in those who had tampered with the flag. He was part of a group of five religious ministers whose respective congregations met at St. Mary's church and paid tribute to Dr. King.

It did not end there. There were letters to the editor in the *Bellevue Press* that further showed local distaste and distrust for Dr. King. One letter, published in the April 25, 1968 edition, lashed out at what the author referred to as misinformed clergy and opportunist politicians for supporting King. It also vehemently labeled Dr. King as having associated with communists and connected this with his antiwar stance on Vietnam. The letter concluded with an attempt at a moderate approach, stating that King did not deserve an assassin's bullet but also did not deserve an official day of mourning either.

No more letters or articles appeared on the subject, although a wanted poster for James Earl Ray would later appear in the newspaper. The year of King's death was also an election year—11,470 residents voted. Of them, 17 percent, or nearly 2,000, marked their ballot for pro-segregationist George Wallace. While we remember the life and efforts of Dr. King, as we move further away from 1968, society often forgets the nuanced attitudes this country faced. Bigotry, ignorance and hatred are and were not exclusive to any one state or region of this country. As uncomfortable as this truth is, sometimes these behaviors can be found much closer to home than we would want them to be.

For an increasing number of people by the end of the 1960s, especially those connected to the military, Sarpy County became home. As Offutt Air Force Base grew in mission and scope, so did the number of base personnel and dependents. In 1960, the first 138 units of Capehart Housing were built. By 1967, there were 1,516 units, with plans for more.

Housing was for both commissioned and noncommissioned officers. Units had either two or three bedrooms, hardwood floors and modern kitchens with appliances, and most units had attached garages with plenty of grassy yards for backyard barbecues. The cost per unit was approximately $13,500. The area included the Capehart Chapel, a 125-bed medical facility, and was served almost exclusively by two Bellevue Public Schools: Peter Sarpy and Fort Crook Elementary. City police and fire provided protection to the more than seven thousand residents of Capehart, and the water supply came from Omaha's municipal system. By 1969, the problem was no longer a housing shortage but rather once again ensuring that there was adequate infrastructure and taxation to support schools, streets, police fire and much more.

The 1970s continued a surge of growth that further blurred the lines between Omaha and nearby Sarpy County. In response to not only new homes but also new neighborhoods and even a newly incorporated municipality during the previous decade, the '70s saw several additional strides in infrastructure, partially in the center of the county. A crowning achievement of the decade was the construction of Midlands Community Hospital.

The hospital has undergone several slight name variations throughout its more than forty-year history. The hospital faced an uphill struggle even before its doors opened on January 12, 1976. The county had been growing at a significant rate since World War II. With the increase in population with Sarpy County and the Omaha metro area as a whole, there was need for a hospital. A year-long study ending in mid-1975 highlighted that sixteen thousand military dependents were hospitalized in Omaha-area facilities—75 percent of those came from the Sarpy County region that Midlands would serve.

Money is linked to healthcare, and the construction of the hospital took a great deal of it in order for the vision to be achieved. A fundraising campaign of $3.1 million ensured that there would be public buy-in. Another $19 million was raised through the issuance tax-free revenue bonds. In addition to coming up with the $22 million needed to construct the hospital, the question of personnel became a point of discussion. The provisional mind-set of the Omaha metropolitan area has been slow to change. In the 1970s, Sarpy County had been one of the fastest-growing areas of Nebraska. Yet the stigma of driving to what many felt was the edge of the earth remained, presenting a powerful concern that Midlands would not be able to recruit the necessary professional talent to sustain a hospital. There were local family physicians and general practitioners, but these were few in number—just eighteen were scattered throughout Sarpy and Cass Counties. Specialists not connected with Offutt were in Omaha. Despite that limited number, the applications came flooding in. A week before the hospital opened, eighty doctors sought staff privileges at Midlands. Support positions were listed daily in the *Omaha World-Herald*.

It was not long before the hospital saw its first patient. The very morning the facility opened, Merle Iske of Papillion was admitted for elective surgery. Not wanting to arrive late, Iske was there when the doors opened at 7:00 a.m. At noon, the doors were closed. The state fire marshal would not give final approval until the cable that led to the automatic alarm system could be connected to the infrastructure that connected into the courthouse. Minor hiccups aside, Midlands, with 208 beds, was five times larger in physical size than its predecessor, Doctors Hospital, and was imbedded within the Sarpy County community so residents did not have to venture into Omaha. Doctors was old-fashioned by the 1970s and the facility lacked an emergency department, whereas Midlands had a separate emergency room entrance, with eight rooms and an additional eight outpatient rooms nearby. An emergency physician was on duty at all times to manage the ward, and its fourteen-member nursing staff could receive two ambulances at a time if need be.

Additional elements of modernity included a modern radiology department. Doctors Hospital had proved too small to allow for such equipment, which would now include an ultrasound machine for expectant mothers. A large coronary care unit to manage patients with heart attacks, angina and various other heart conditions was another prominent aspect of the hospital. With more hospital beds and an increase in outpatients, a larger laboratory meant that a wider range of medical tests could be completed. Finally, the hospital contained four floors of patient rooms. Similar to other area hospitals, the semi-private rooms were seventy-five dollars per day—for an additional ten dollars, a patient could have a private room. Free parking facilities for up to six hundred cars and an adjacent medical office building rounded out the grounds.

A second noteworthy occurrence was that after more than fifty years of steady service, the 11,423-square-foot courthouse was proving to be outdated in both size and scope. Construction of the new and present courthouse along with the hall of justice was begun in September 1971. In 1973, with the hall of justice complete, the county began transitioning from old building to new. Work on the courthouse was completed in July 1974, and both buildings were dedicated on May 4, 1975.

At 43,395 square feet, the facility was nearly four times the size of the old courthouse. The modern building contained ample room for elected officials, their staff and their respective records. It took the voters of Sarpy County several attempts to approve the bond issue in order for the courthouse to be built, but a positive outcome of the larger building was that Papillion gained the old courthouse as its city hall.

Throughout the 1970s and into the 1980s, Sarpy County, especially the eastern part, became the backdrop for quintessential suburban America. Communities in Sarpy County had long been trustful and relatively innocent places to reside. People largely left their doors unlocked. Youth who were caught partaking in underage drinking were more likely to get a ride home from the sheriff or police and a much worse punishment from angry parents than a judge could legally provide. Younger kids were free to roam so long as they headed home when the streetlights turned on for the evening. While Sarpy County and its communities were not a utopian, crime-free society, in the mind of the public heinous crime was committed elsewhere—certainly not here.

That unfortunately changed in the fall of 1983. In the early morning hours of September 18, 1983, Danny Joe Eberle set off on his bicycle to begin his morning newspaper route in Bellevue. The thirteen-year-old only

There were several failed attempts to construct a new courthouse, including this 1963–64 rendering, before the present-day facility was built. *Sarpy County Museum.*

delivered three of his seventy newspapers before he vanished, leaving his bike and remaining papers at the fourth house.

Following a detailed search, his body was found three days later in a grassy ditch about four miles south of Bellevue. It was abundantly clear that he had been abducted. The FBI joined the efforts of the Bellevue police and the Sarpy County Sheriff's Office to investigate. Their leads were soon exhausted, and the trail went cold.

The murderer struck again on December 2, 1983, when twelve-year-old Christopher Walden disappeared while walking to school. Walden's body was found two days after his abduction five miles south of Papillion by pheasant hunters. This time, witnesses were able to provide a partial description, focusing on a white male driving a tan car.

The public remained on edge. It was clear that there was a serial child murderer on the loose. Children were no longer allowed to walk to school or roam unsupervised without an adult. Posters containing a composite sketch of the suspect were spread throughout Sarpy County. In addition to investigating, the sheriff's office maintained a high physical presence in the hopes of deterring another murder. Sarpy County sheriff Pat Thomas appealed to the media, but rather than issue a passionate plea for the killer to cease, he openly taunted and mocked the unknown murderer. Sheriff Thomas told him that if were watching, that he was a "coward who could only kill children" and that "if he were a real man, he would stop picking on children and start picking on someone his own size." The tactic worked. The killer was paying attention, and he was enraged.

Five weeks after the Walden abduction, a third attempt took place. On the early morning of January 11, 1984, a preschool teacher was getting ready for the day before her students arrived at Aldersgate United Methodist Church. The teacher, Barbara Weaver, had seen a car circling the church before the driver stopped, exited the car and walked up to the door. It was there that she stood face to face with John Joubert. Both parties knew that the conversation they were about to have was under false pretenses. After a brief exchange, his friendly demeanor suddenly turned sinister. Weaver was able to flee, but not before she managed to remember the license plate of the car, including its county prefix of 59, the designated number for a vehicle registered in Sarpy County.

The car was traced back to a car dealership. It had been provided to Joubert while his car, a Chevy Nova, was undergoing repairs. The knowledge of the plate number was a crucial lead that traced the Nova to Airman Joubert, stationed at Offutt Air Force Base. Acting on information from the Sarpy County Sheriff's Office, a Bellevue police officer along with an FBI agent met with members of the air force's Office of Security and Investigation to search the young airman's dorm room. Inside, they found the boyish-looking twenty-year-old fast asleep, along with physical evidence. The young man, who had been an assistant Scoutmaster with a local Boy Scout troop, was hardly the physical embodiment of the mental image that many had of a monster.

Soon after, Joubert confessed to the murders. He admitted to an additional murder of an eleven-year-old in Maine prior to his arrival at Offutt AFB. A three-judge panel found Joubert guilty. He was sentenced to death in the electric chair, which was carried out on July 17, 1996. The chapter marked the moment when innocence was lost. It is perhaps the darkest time in Sarpy County's history, but one that should not be omitted and hopefully never repeated.

The communities in Sarpy County sought to move forward after this. The 1980s and '90s were full of summers that included Bellevue's Arrows to Aerospace; Papillion, Gretna and Springfield Days; and, for years, La

The initial photo of Joubert at the time he was taken into custody by Bellevue police. His description—five-foot-six, 135 pounds, hazel eyes and brown hair—is on the reverse. *Sarpy County Museum.*

Vista Daze. There were airshows from the base and the Sarpy County Fair. New homes, even entire neighborhoods and new schools, continued to be constructed. Widening and paving of roads and installation of streetlights took place. In many ways, what was old was new again, as much of Sarpy County's history can be circular. What development and change had happened in Bellevue decades earlier was quickly starting to take hold elsewhere in the county as well, particularly in Papillion and central Sarpy County.

Global events once again connected to Sarpy County when, following the collapse of the Soviet Union, the United States reorganized aspects of its military, including Strategic Air Command. SAC had remained at Offutt for forty-four years, until 1992. As emerging post–Cold War threats came into view, a command structure to address these concerns was put into place. In the wake of the collapse of the Soviet Union, a new command, the United States Strategic Command (USSTRATCOM), succeeded SAC in a rapidly changing world. USSTRATCOM was established on June 1, 1992, with the purpose of streamlining the command and control of the United States' strategic nuclear arsenal. Both leaders of the United States and Russia came to understandings on strategic nuclear armaments. Around the time these treaties—known as Strategic Arms Reduction Treaty (START) I and START II—were taking place, General George Butler was assigned to command the newly minted USSTRATCOM at Offutt.

This new unified command oversaw air force bombers, intercontinental ballistic missiles and intercontinental nuclear-armed missiles launched from navy submarines. The joint effort between the air force and navy was made up of nearly 2,900 personnel at its onset, of which one-third were navy. However, similar to the era of SAC, the ultimate goal remained nuclear deterrence. If that failed, however, it was the job of USSTRATCOM to employ this nation's nuclear weaponry.

Cooperation between the United States and Russia, the holders of the two largest nuclear stockpiles in the world, became a paramount characteristic of USSTRATCOM. In the years following General Butler's change of command, Admiral Henry Chiles, General Eugene Habiger and Admiral Richard Mies continued the efforts of threat reduction to national and global security through cooperation. However, new threats were emerging on the cusp of the twenty-first century, threats stemming from rogue nations or even stateless terrorists.

Those threats would become a reality on a dark day in September 2001. As the events of September 11, 2001, transpired, President George W. Bush was taken to Offutt and into the secure command center for USSTRATCOM. He would not remain there very long, a little over an hour, but it was long enough for the fog of war to begin to recede. Present Bush's decision to come to Offutt that day reconfirmed Offutt's key role in national security.

Epilogue

THE SILICON PRAIRIE

The history of Sarpy County continues to be written. The land remains ever present, but new schools, housing developments and businesses continue to be built. The agriculture scene, with its gravel roads interspersed with rustic barns and farmhouses that dot the landscape, are becoming a distant memory as urban sprawl continues to shift into Sarpy County. There was once a prairie with a century-old family farmstead, but now there resides a silicon prairie with a data center for a Fortune 500 company.

Bellevue, which saw far more development decades ahead of the other Sarpy County communities, continues to remain the largest city in Sarpy County. It has suffered in recent years from Missouri River flooding but has not been set back in its construction of a new police station and city hall, and it is attempting to take great strides to redevelop aspects of Olde Towne Bellevue, built in haste in the years following World War II. Bellevue has more than 150 years of history and the prospect to continue to add to that narrative.

At present, Gretna has been the fastest-growing city in Nebraska since the year 2000. Its future, in many ways, mirrors the growth of Bellevue during the 1940s and '50s. The historical relevancy of Gretna's location holds just as true today as it did when it was established. Right off I-80, between Lincoln and Omaha, Gretna as of 2010 had a population of just over 4,400, a figure that was likely outdated before the 2010 census results were released.

La Vista has continued to bloom, and despite a few growing pains, it has gained a police station, a second fire station, a large library coupled with Metro Community College, sleek retail, a convention center, hotels, restaurants, a movie theater and shopping. The 1960s town has annexed well beyond its original borders. In fact, between 1995 and 2007, there were eighteen separate annexations to the city. As the original new city smell has now worn off the sixty-year-old community, it has carved out a downtown for the twenty-first century through the Corridor 84 project, a transformative plan to renovate La Vista's section of Eighty-Fourth Street as a destination rather than a drive-through community.

Of course, Offutt Air Force Base cannot be forgotten. While the Glenn L. Martin Bomber Plant cost $10.8 million and the Pentagon had an $83 million price tag in 1940 and 1941, respectively, the colossal $1.3 billion USSTRATCOM building will ensure that the United States can tackle twenty-first-century threats. In addition to the vital and continued mission of the Fifty-Fifth Wing, there are dozens of partner units hosted at Offutt. The Defense POW/MIA Accounting Agency has a professional lab in the depths of Building D, the old bomber plant facility. Here teams of scientists, anthropologists, historians and other professionals help locate, identify and provide closure for those fallen service men and women, as well as their families. Offutt has had a versatile but vital role in history and will continue to do so in the future.

Papillion has continued to thrive in recent years. Home to the Kansas City Royals Triple A affiliate at Werner Park, Prairie Queen and Walnut Creek Recreation Areas, Sumpter Amphitheater and, recently, Papillion Landing Community Center, Papillion has routinely been ranked one of the best places to live. The silhouettes of long-standing farm silos have been replaced with housing subdivisions.

Finally, Springfield, the smallest town in Sarpy County, has perhaps the largest future potential. As the final frontier to Sarpy County, Springfield offers great quality of life and the Sarpy County Fair and is poised to become an increasingly thriving community with a strong school system. Will it maintain its small-town atmosphere with rural roots, or will it evolve as the landscape of Sarpy County does?

Much of what has transpired here has been successful due to the collaboration between residents and elected officials at the city, county, state and even federal levels. For now, Sarpy County remains a hybrid, a mix of rural and urban, but for how much longer? The five Sarpy County communities continue to grow, annexing land that was once strictly under the aegis of the county. It is not inconceivable that one day, all but a slim selection of plots of land will be directly overseen by the cities of Sarpy County.

Werner Park was built in 2011 for the Omaha Storm Chasers, formerly the Omaha Royals, when they moved from Rosenblatt Stadium into Sarpy County. *Sarpy County Museum.*

A new chapter of Sarpy County history is being written at present. What will the story of today tell the forthcoming residents of Sarpy County and its communities? What events, occurrences, triumphs and tragedies will make the history books? Who will be included in the narrative, and who will be omitted? How will one consider nearly two hundred years of history? These are all questions that will have to be addressed by future historians, who undoubtedly will delve into fragments of digital files, unsubstantiated social media information, bits of surviving paper and perhaps even through Freedom of Information Act requests. With proper foresight, Sarpy County, its communities and their people can ensure that the history of the present will be suitably told for future generations.

BIBLIOGRAPHY

Agricultural Extension News Service. "Boys Get Training for Farm or Navy" (July 1944).

Bangs, S.D. *S.D. Bangs' Centennial History of Sarpy County*. Papillion, NE: Papillion Times Print, 1876.

Beaumont, Mitch. *Creating a Community: La Vista 50 Years*. La Vista: City of La Vista, Nebraska, 2009.

Bellevue Gazette. "Local and Miscellaneous." August 6, 1857.

Bellevue Press. "Mayor Backs Newspaper Policy." December 7, 1945.

Bighia, Dave. "History of Offutt AFB." *History of Offutt AFB*. Bellevue, NE: Sarpy County Museum, 1994.

A Bridge from the Past: Papillion, Nebraska, 1870–1970. Papillion, NE, 1970.

Charvat, Charles. *Logan Fontenelle: An Indian Chief in Broadcloth and Fine Linen, a Biographical Narrative, by Charles Charvat*. Omaha, NE, 1961.

Christianson, Gale E. *Last Posse: A Jailbreak, a Manhunt, and the End of Hang-Em-High Justice*. Guilford, CT: Lyons Press, 2001.

Clark, William, and Meriwether Lewis. *The Journals of Lewis and Clark*. London: Penguin Books, 2002.

Dries, Angelyn. *Be Centered in Christ and Not in Self: The Missionary Society of Saint Columban, the North American Story (1918–2018)*. St. Columbans, NE: Missionary Society of St. Columban, 2017.

Gale, Kira. *Peter A. Sarpy & Early Bellevue*. Omaha, NE: River Junction Press, 1999.

Giese, Rhea. *View of a Century in Sarpy County*. Sarpy County, NE, 1967.

Goss, Charles Chaucer. *Bellevue, Larimer & Saint Mary: Their History, Location, Description and Advantages*. Bellevue, NE: John Q. Goss, 1859.

Grayson, Deb. *Papillion: A City on Track*. N.p.: Suburban Newspapers Inc., 2005.

Hillabrand, Robert, Lloyd Schoolfield, Jen Wheeler, Sally Mackeprang and Monty Daganaar. *The History of the Sarpy County Sheriff's Office: 150 Years of History 1857–2007*. N.p., n.d.

The History of Fort Crook, 1888 Offutt Air Force Base, 1976. Omaha, NE, 1981.

Justman, Ben. *Bellevue*. Charleston, SC: Arcadia Publishing, 2011.

———. *Offutt Air Force Base*. Charleston, SC: Arcadia Publishing, 2014.

Kearns, Edward F. *History of Papillion, Nebraska*. N.p., 1962.

Lewis, Linda. *Moses Merrill Would Be Impressed!: A History of Education in Bellevue, Nebraska*. Bellevue, NE: Bellevue Public School System, 1978.

Lienemann, Donald H. *Miracles Do Happen: A B-17 Navigators Story of the September 11, 1944, Mission to Destroy the Ruhland, Germany Oil Refinery and His Prison Camp Experience in Stalag Luft I*. Kearney, NE: Morris Publishing, 2003.

Nebraska Palladium. "The Nebraska." March 21, 1855.

Old Bellevue. Papillion, NE: Papillion Times, 1954.

Omaha Daily Bee. "Military Aid and Masonic Rites for Delanney." December 30, 1918.

Omaha World-Herald. "Backs WPA Jobs at Fort." August 1, 1938.

———. "Carload of Alcohol Will Go Into Sewer." June 30, 1928.

———. "Federal Attorney Will Visit Hutter; 3 New Arrests." August 11, 1931.

———. "McCauley Headed Biggest Labor Program." March 3, 1939.

———. "Midlands Hospital, Bigger and Better to Open Jan. 12." January 5, 1976.

———. "Sarpy WPA Crew Strikes." December 11, 1935.

———. "Say Found with Booze." May 25, 1928.

———. "Start New School at Pleasant Hill." December 21, 1938.

———. "WPA Reports on Work Done in 3 Counties." December 20, 1936.

Papillion Times. "County Extension Program Shows Accomplishments." January 7, 1943.

———. "Court House Falling Apart." November 10, 1921.

———. "Sarpy County Historical Society Appeals to People of County." June 18, 1936.

———. "State Board Issues Order." October 24, 1918.

Pettit, Mark. *A Need to Kill*. New York: Ballantine, 1991.
Podoll, Dean. *Civil War Veterans Buried in Sarpy County*. Bellevue, NE: Sarpy County Museum, 2012.
Scouting Our Story. Omaha, NE: Mid-America Council Boy Scouts of America, 2010.
Shallcross, William John. *Romance of a Village: Story of Bellevue, the First Permanent Continuous Settlement in Nebraska*. Omaha, NE: Roncka Bros., printers, 1954.
Simmons, Jerold L. *La Belle Vue: Studies in the History of Bellevue, Nebraska*. Bellevue, NE: Jerold L. Simmons, 1976.
———. "Public Leadership in a World War II Boom Town: Bellevue, Nebraska." *Nebraska History* 65 (1984): 484–99.
Springfield at Its Source, 1882–1982. Springfield, NE: The Committee, 1982.
Village of Bellevue Meeting Minutes. Sarpy County Museum Archives, Bellevue, Nebraska.

ABOUT THE SARPY COUNTY MUSEUM

Located at 2402 Clay Street in Bellevue, the Sarpy County Museum is dedicated to protecting, promoting and preserving the history of Sarpy County, its communities and their people. Dating back to 1934, the organization served as the "Smithsonian of Sarpy County." Staff and volunteers serve as docents, work with collections, prepare displays, facilitate programs and ensure that the rich history of Sarpy County does not fade away.

The museum features several rotating exhibits to augment the permanent displays. The collection includes artifacts, government records, newspapers, historical documents, photographs and a variety of resources, all of which are available to the public. Rather than leave items in an attic, basement or with a family member unsure about what to save, the museum strongly encourages people to share anything that might be historically or culturally significant to Sarpy County. If you're not sure what's important, staff would be glad to chat.

Additionally, several historic properties—including Bellevue's 1830s Log Cabin, the Burlington Railroad Depot, the Union Pacific Caboose and Moses Merrill Mission site—are affiliated with the museum. The cabin, depot and caboose have been preserved to nearly their original condition. All sites are available for tours.

Primary support to fund these endeavors gratefully comes from Sarpy County, grants, fundraisers, memberships and donations from readers and supporters. As the museum is a small nonprofit 501(c)(3) organization with a big mission, these financial efforts allow the museum to continue to save local history.

The Sarpy County Museum is on Facebook and Twitter and can be contacted at 402-292-1880 or director@sarpymuseum.org. The museum is open Tuesday through Saturday from 10:00 a.m. to 4:00 p.m. We hope to see you soon!